Clue®

MYSTERIES

15 WHODUNITS TO SOLVE IN MINUTES

BY VICKI CAMERON

Viva Books Private Limited
New Delhi • Mumbai • Chennai • Kolkata • Bangalore

First Indian Edition 2004

VIVA BOOKS PRIVATE LIMITED

- 4262/3 Ansari Road, Daryaganj, New Delhi 110 002
  E-mail: viva@vivagroupindia.net
- 215-216 New Apollo Estate, 2nd Floor, Mogra Lane, Andheri (E), Mumbai 400 069
  E-mail: vivamumbai@vivagroupindia.net
- Jamal Fazal Chambers, 26 Greams Road, Chennai 600 0067
  E-mail: vivachennai@vivagroupindia.net
- B-103, Jindal Towers, 21/1A/3, Darga Road, Kolkata-700 017
  E-mail: vivakolkata@vivagroupindia.net
- 7 GF, Sovereign Park Apts., 56-58 K. R. Road, Basavanagudi, Bangalore 560 004
  Email: vivabangalore@vivagroupindia.net

Published by arrangement with

Running Press Book Publishers
A Member of the Perseus Books LLC
Eleven Cambridge Center
Cambridge MA 02142
USA

ISBN 81-7649-877-7

Published by Vinod Vasishtha for Viva Books Private Limited, 4262/3 Ansari Road, New Delhi 110 002 and printed at Print Perfect, New Delhi.

Contents

An Invitation to Tudor Hall

Shysters and bounders, gold-diggers and con artists. Tudor Hall would soon be full of them, judging by the wad of letters in Mrs. White's hand.

"Good morning, Master Boddy," Mrs. White said as she entered the study. "The post is here." She placed the letters on his desk and stood back, arms folded over her white apron. "Are you quite looking forward to your birthday party?"

"I've been looking forward to it since Uncle Hugh died in 1914." *Twelve years of living on an allowance.* "I wonder which of our potential guests will be able to visit for a fortnight." John Boddy slit open the first envelope, scented lavender with a feather printed in the corner. "Do I smell smoke from the kitchen?"

"Surely not. There are scones in the oven, but they've ten minutes yet. Or is it ten minutes total? No, I'm sure they're not ready."

John sighed. Mrs. White had been keeping house for his uncle Sir Hugh, and now for him, for over thirty years, but she still didn't quite have the knack of the Aga cooker. He read the first letter.

Dear John,

I would be delighted to attend your upcoming birthday party. I happen to be free all summer so I can stay as long as you like. I shall arrive from London by train on the third of June. Please have a car pick me up at the station.

Regards

(Mrs.) Patricia Peacock

"That's the first, then. Mrs. Peacock has accepted. She'll be here tomorrow. Do you have the rooms ready?" Boddy checked the name off his list. *Mrs. Peacock.*

"I've done nothing but clean rooms and change beds since you came up with this birthday party idea. I've got out the best china, too. Is she bringing one of her husbands with her?"

"No, she isn't married at present. Her last husband died nine years ago."

"Oh. So she's running out of money."

"I'm sure Sir Matthew left her well provided for."

"You ought to spend a little less time reading archeological journals and a little more time reading the tabloids. That woman spends money faster than stink fills a room."

"Speaking of stink, I am positive I smell smoke."

"The scones are not baked yet, and that's a fact."

Boddy shrugged. He never knew quite how to take Mrs. White. She'd baffled him as a nanny and she baffled him as a housekeeper and cook. She was fanatic about order and outward appearance, but didn't notice smoke billowing from the oven. He opened the next letter, written on French deckle edge pink notepaper.

Dear John,

Happy birthday! I suppose you will be inheriting all that lovely money. That's what Mother says. Thirty seems so old. Anyway, I'd love to come to the party. I'm in a play here but it might close earlier than expected so I'll be free to come after the first of June. You will send me a train ticket, won't you, darling?

Josephine Scarlet

"That's another acceptance. Miss Scarlet is coming." Boddy checked the next name off the list. *Miss Scarlet*. "She wants me to send her a train ticket. Do you think she'll still come if I don't?"

"She's a right burden, that one," Mrs. White said. "Happen as not she'll come and stay all summer, mooching off your hospitality."

"I'm sure she's a fine young lady."

"You've not been reading the tabloids, then. You want to watch yourself. She's near your age, and not a suitable catch."

"I haven't seen her for over five years. I understand she's become quite beautiful."

"Aye, she's that. Looks just like your mother, rest her soul."

Boddy sliced open the next envelope and extracted a letter written on plain white paper with regimental letterhead. He read it aloud.

Boddy:

Capital idea. Will be there. Arriving on the third instant. Driving down from London.

Colonel M. Mustard, Retired

Mrs. White smiled. "The colonel's coming, then? I do admire the colonel. All those medals."

All that hot air, too, Boddy thought, but checked off the name on his list. *Colonel Mustard.* "Uncle Hugh once told me Mustard didn't come by his medals by heroism."

"Sir Hugh liked to make things work to his advantage. He'd tell you anything if he'd profit."

"How would he profit from a tale like that?"

"I don't know, but the colonel will explain it, I'm sure."

"I'm afraid he will. Several times."

The next letter was quite plain with a green border.

My dear Mr. Boddy,

I am delighted to accept your invitation to spend a fortnight at Tudor Hall. May the Higher Power continue to bless you with birthdays. I have a business opportunity I know you will be interested in, particularly after the last restriction of Sir Hugh's will is lifted from the estate.

Blessings of Heaven on you.

Mr. J. Green

"Mr. Green will be coming."

"Humph. I'd better count the silver, then."

"Really, Mrs. White. He's a man of the cloth."

"Surely you don't really believe that? He's no more of a Reverend than you or me. He never graduated from that American seminary he attended. I just don't know how he fools anybody."

"Uncle Hugh liked him, though."

"Sir Hugh and Green did a lot of business together. Liking wasn't a factor."

The last letter was written on stationery bearing the coat of arms of the British Museum.

Dear Boddy,

Thank you for the invitation to the Tudor Hall party. I'm at loose ends at the moment, so this is perfect. I'm sure I'll be able to catch a lift down with someone. I wonder if we could have a talk while I'm there about another Egyptian expedition I have in mind. I know Sir Hugh would have approved of it.

P. Plum

"Plum is coming."

"I should expect so. Turned out on his ear, he is, from the British Museum. He'll be looking for a handout."

"That's all of them, then." Boddy checked off the last two names on his list. *Mr. Green. Professor Plum.* "They'll all be here."

"Good thing it isn't a surprise party," Mrs. White said.

"Oh, I have some surprises for them," Boddy replied. "They've all been on a free ride on Uncle Hugh's generosity, living beyond their means because of the monthly allowances in his will. Those conditions cease on my thirtieth birthday. I've been giving a lot of thought to what to do with the estate when it's all mine, unencumbered. There will be many surprises on June eighteenth."

He pushed the acceptance letters into a stack and dropped them in the wastebasket. Scoundrels and charlatans, prima donnas and wastrels. *Happy birthday to me.*

Carte Blanche

Mrs. Blanche White lined up the Royal Worcester cups and saucers on the silver tray on the tea trolley and stood beside it, waiting for the guests to arrive for four o'clock tea.

Mrs. Peacock fluttered in, scattering pinfeathers from her velvet cloche hat. "Mrs. White, please have the upstairs maid bring me fresh towels before dinner."

"There's no upstairs maid, right enough. Sir Hugh didn't like a lot of servants underfoot, just me and my husband Winslow, the chauffeur, rest his soul. Now there's just me, cook, housekeeper, and nanny to Master John when he was young." She smoothed her white apron over her black uniform. "So you'll be having fresh towels when I get to it. Would you care for tea?"

Mrs. Peacock perched on the edge of the chintz chesterfield, her legs neatly crossed at the ankles. Her stylish cobalt blue suit matched her hat. Everything about her was some shade of blue, from the necklace-earrings-bracelet suite to the eye makeup and shoes. Like as not her blood ran blue. The fox stole looked a mite peculiar. Not quite right for teatime. She must want to impress the other guests. Mrs. Peacock had always been fussy during her visits, insisting her pillow be fluffed just so, with an arched eyebrow for emphasis, and herself with six more beds to make.

As the remaining guests straggled into the lounge, Mrs. White poured each one a cup of tea and offered a plate of homemade shortbread, her best Scottish dish, baked from a recipe handed down in the Chaulkley family for six generations. She was right proud of her baking, and she'd left all the burned ones in the kitchen.

Colonel Mustard leaned against the mantel, his medals shining on his immaculate khaki uniform. His hair had turned white since his last visit, but he still had the mutton chop sideburns and bushy moustache. She'd find his room in crisp order when she went to do it up, from the tight corners on the sheets to the polished shoes lined up against the baseboard.

Mr. Green commandeered one of the green leather armchairs, his tailored hunter-green suit falling in perfect lines and creases and his wingtip shoes gleaming. Too smooth by half, that one. His hair, what there was of it, was pomaded into a sheen. His shirt was crisply white. There'd be a job for her, no doubt, doing his ironing. His tie matched his suit and the whole outfit looked like something Sir Hugh would have bought in Italy. None of the finery covered up the shifty look in his eyes. She didn't trust him as far as she could throw him, never had.

Professor Plum relaxed into the other armchair, his purple tweed jacket appearing two sizes too large and allowing the chair to swallow him. His bow tie was askew over a rumpled shirt. His wire-rim glasses sat tilted on his nose, as if he'd sat on them and bent the frame. Like as not he'd be one to leave things lying around. She'd have to keep a sharp eye.

The lounge was quiet save for the tinkling of spoons in four saucers. The tension in the room made the hairs on the Oriental rug stand on end. The only movement was the flickering sun through the tall casement windows and the exchanging of thin smiles. Master Boddy had better arrive soon or his guests would expire of awkwardness.

"I don't believe we all know each other," Mrs. Peacock said. "Or at least, some of us haven't met for several years. Perhaps we ought to introduce ourselves."

The gentlemen offered vague nods of agreement.

"I am Mrs. Patricia Peacock, my late husband was Sir Matthew Peacock, you may have heard of him. He was a noted barrister in London. I've known Sir Hugh Black since 1900, although I only met his nephew John Boddy once or twice. He was always away at boarding school when I visited Sir Hugh. I do like to travel abroad; one gets so tired of English rain." She fluttered a hand toward the window, and all the feathers on her hat quivered. "I am particularly fond of shopping in Paris. The styles are so youthful."

A right twit, that one, pushing fifty and passing for forty. Mrs. White considered offering Mrs. Peacock more shortbread, but her kind was always watching their weight.

"Colonel Michael Mustard here. Formerly with the Royal Hampshire Regiment, known as the Fighting Tigers. Army family, father was a captain, sent me to military school. Served in Africa and the Middle East. Been decorated, as you can see." He pointed to the row of medals on his uniform. "Left the Tigers, assigned to military intelligence. All hush-hush, I shall speak no more about it. Retired after the Great War. Writing my memoirs. Lifelong member of the Magniloquent Club in London. That is all." He nodded at them, like a commander who has just given a summary of the battle to his superior officer, and drained his cup.

Mrs. White poured him a fresh cup. Nice man, one you could rely on in a pinch. About her age, too, sixty if he was a day.

"We shall have lots in common, I see. I'm Professor Peter Plum. I studied ancient Mid-Eastern culture at Oxford and taught there for a number of years. I spent my summers overseeing archeological expeditions in Egypt. Our family used to live there, you see, and I've many happy childhood memories of playing in the sand. For the last three years I've worked for the British Museum. I'm between jobs, at the moment, taking a rest from the museum, negotiating my next archeology dig. Boddy invited me to spend the summer here, and it seemed like an excellent idea. I shall so enjoy getting to know you all."

Mrs. White kept her arms folded while Plum searched his saucer for the shortbread he'd already eaten. Professor Prat, more likely. She'd heard a thing or two about him, and 'taking a rest from the museum' was a bit of a lean away from the truth. Fired was more like it.

"I'm Mr. John Green. I studied in America, at Praise and Glory Seminary. I don't have a parish. I'm more of an itinerant preacher. I've been all over England, the Continent, and Africa, praise be, helping those who seek." He lifted his spoon from his saucer and waved it in the air.

Mrs. White looked down at her feet. It was a struggle to keep a straight face when someone was giving the benediction of the teaspoon. She'd better go around with the shortbread plate again right smartly or he'd be having them down on their knees singing hymns. She picked up the tray and headed straight for the professor. He took three pieces, one for each hand and one for the saucer.

The door swept open and a beautiful young woman in a scarlet evening gown paused under the arch and swept her eyes around the room. She was so radiant she glittered, from her tousled brown hair past her deep red lips to her manicured toenails in high-heeled sandals. Mrs. White wondered if the lass knew how overdressed she was for tea. Mr. Green stood up. Colonel Mustard straightened up. Professor Plum looked confused, no, stunned.

"Where's John?" she asked with a tiny pout.

"This is my daughter, Miss Josephine Scarlet." Mrs. Peacock said. "Late, as usual."

"Really, Mother, I'm sure they all know me. Everyone goes to the theatre in the West End. I was in *The Importance of Being Frank*, and *She Stoops to Commiserate.* Not the lead roles, but my name was in lights." She sashayed to the chesterfield and sat down with a sweep of her train.

Three heads shook 'no'. The Reverend sat down and the Colonel returned to his at-ease position. Professor Plum did not remember to close his mouth.

"Well, after that I went to America, to Hollywood. I played lead in a major film, *Ben Hur*. Unfortunately, their funding was cancelled or something, so Blake said, he was the assistant director, and they had to halt production."

"I saw that film," Colonel Mustard said. "Capital action scenes. First class fighting."

"Scarlet. Didn't I see your name in the tabloids?" Mr. Green stroked his chin. "Something to do with Sir Humphrey Ponsonby-Smythe and a deathbed wedding?"

"All untrue, I assure you. He was dead before the minister arrived. I don't know where the press gets such notions. Anyway, I'm through with old men. I'm going to spend some time getting to know John Boddy this summer. Especially after his birthday, when he inherits all this." She waved her hand at the ornate stucco ceiling and silk damask walls. "This mansion and grounds. And all the money that goes with it."

Mrs. White straightened the sugar bowl on the tray. If that empty-headed young tart wanted to wangle her way into Master Boddy's attentions, she had better bone up. Upper-class twit. Master John was graduated from the University of Oxford with a doctorate in Anthropology. He didn't have much time for frippery.

"Where's John?" Miss Scarlet asked again. "He should be here by now. I'll have to go out and come in again."

"Unavoidably detained, I should expect," Colonel Mustard said. "Reminds me of the time we were waiting for the General in the Sudan. It had been a hot, tiring day, and we'd suffered several casualties. We were waiting further instructions from the general and his entourage was two hours overdue. Started thinking 'ambush', we did."

"Quite so," Mrs. Peacock interrupted. "Josephine, where did you get that dress? It's quite stunning on you."

"Dropped shoulders are the work of the devil," Mr. Green said, brandishing his spoon at Miss Scarlet. "Red is the color of Lucifer. Repent or your soul will wallow in the florid flames of--"

"I don't know who Lucy Fur is, but this gown was designed by Lily Levere, and she uses all shades of red, so I don't think this Lucy Fur person can hold claim to it." Miss Scarlet smoothed the bodice of the gown in question.

Professor Plum watched said bodice until his Adam's apple bobbed. "We don't wear much red in Egypt. Lots of white, for the heat, you know." He pushed his glasses straighter and gestured at Mrs. White for a refill of tea.

"The Sudan is every bit as hot, yet we waited for the General through the day and into the night. The men were worn out waiting. We finally set up a watch so the rest of us could get some kip."

"Sleep? Is that what governs you when you're out battling a righteous fight against the heathen hordes?" Mr. Green pointed his accusing spoon at the colonel. "A man should not rest until the last recalcitrant is brought into the fold."

"Fold? I think Blamand does a better job with folds than Fuleaux, especially when it comes to silk, although Fuleaux's satin folds are quite acceptable." Miss Scarlet nibbled at the corner of her shortbread. "Is there butter in these? I have to watch how much butter I eat."

"You can't make a decent shortbread without butter, miss, I'm sure." Mrs. White smiled. One must always be polite. What did she think shortbread was made with? Mutton fat?

"We'd have given our eye teeth for butter on a little bit of bread while we were waiting for the General."

"How long will we be waiting for John Boddy?" Miss Scarlet swept the shortbread crumbs off her lap onto the chesterfield cushions. "I'm finding this quite boring."

Colonel Mustard tapped his riding crop against his knee. "If you will excuse me." He bowed to the ladies and left the room.

"What shall we do while we wait for Mr. Boddy?" Mrs. Peacock asked. "How about a rousing game of charades? If that doesn't offend you, Reverend."

"No, I quite enjoy parlor games," Mr. Green said. "Here's one." He made the hand signal for 'book', held up one finger, then thumped one fist hard against his other palm.

"Bible," Professor Plum guessed. "Jolly good. Try another. Here's one." He held up nine fingers and gestured 'book'. He got up and lumbered around the room, bent over, peering through an imaginary magnifying glass.

"The Great Detective Solves a Case?" Mrs. Peacock guessed. "The Hunchback of Notre-Dame?"

"No, and no," Plum said.

"I don't have a guess," Miss Scarlet said. "I give up."

Mr. Green sighed and left the room.

Plum shrugged. "*Treasures of Tutankhamun's Tomb in the Valley of Kings*. Perhaps you haven't read that one." He returned to his seat.

"I hate charades. But I do have experience as an entertainer. Shall I sing for you?" Miss Scarlet stood up and cleared her throat. *"Aaaahhhhhhh, Sweeeeet Mystereeeee of--"*

A bang and a crash echoed from somewhere in the house.

Miss Scarlet giggled. "My voice is breaking crystal again. I hope it wasn't a large piece. Where was I? Oh yes, *Mystereeee of Somethiiiing Somethiiiing at Last I've Flung Youoooooo*."

"I rather enjoy charades," Professor Plum said. "Let me guess, that was song title, any number of words. I believe the rules are that you can't use actual words, only gestures, so could you do that again, without making sounds? I think I might be able to solve it. Especially if you give me the word count."

Colonel Mustard reappeared in the room. "Mr. Boddy will not be joining us this evening. Where was I? Ah, yes, getting a little kip while we waited for the General."

"Kip Waiting for the General. Is this a song title or a book?" Plum asked. "You missed my reminder of the rules, that you don't use actual words, just gestures."

Mr.Green wandered back in. "Who's doing the shooting? Is there a hunt in the neighborhood?"

"Hunt? Do you think it might be Clarke Hunt? He's quite dishy." Miss Scarlet swayed to the window and peered over the lawns. "I don't see anyone."

Mrs. White picked up her tray and took it to the kitchen. Let them play their silly games. She had the washing up to do. They'd eaten most of the shortbread. She'd planned on making the batch last a week, but now she'd have to bake again.

When she had cleared up in the kitchen, wiped the butcher's block and swept the tiled floor, she did a tidy-tour of the rooms before starting dinner. In the conservatory, two leaves had fallen from the aspidistra. She tucked them into the plant's pot. In the billiard room, someone had left the balls scattered. She racked them, and twitched the taupe drapes closed so the sun wouldn't fade the green baize. In the library, someone had left two revolvers on the reading table. She replaced them in the wall display, aligned the dailies, and closed some open books.

On the library floor, someone had left the body of John Boddy, shot through the heart. How untidy. How thoughtless. The house would be in an uproar for hours while the police clumped around in big dirty boots. She'd have to work overtime cleaning up, with no one to notice and put a bonus in her pay packet. Who could have done this to her?

She marched to the lounge. Mustard leaned on the mantel, explaining something about regimental marching orders. Green sat stroking his Bible, his eyes glazed over. Through the window she could see the other three in the garden, pointing at something moving in the woods. She paused under the arch of the door as Miss Scarlet had done; the occasion seemed to call for added drama.

"I accuse you of shooting Mr. Boddy with the revolver in the library."

Carte Blanche

Solution:

"I did not," Green protested. "I am a man of the cloth. I uphold the sanctity of life, etceteras."

"I didn't mean you."

"I should think not. I am wounded to the core at the mere suggestion." He stalked from the room, his white wingtip shoes whistling over the hardwood.

Mrs. White faced Colonel Mustard and wagged her finger. "I meant you. You said Master Boddy would not be joining us for tea. You knew that because you knew he was dead. Because you shot him."

Colonel Mustard tapped his riding crop on the floor.

"And well he deserved it, too. Bringing me here with the promise of a summer respite, then saddling me with buffoons as conversation companions. I try to relate an interesting incident from the battlefield, and they don't listen. They want to talk of trifles. That's tantamount to treason. Treason, I say. Called him out on it. Challenged him to a duel. Selected two weapons from the display on the wall. Loaded them. Offered him the choice. He just laughed. Handed him the better weapon, took ten paces, turned, and shot. Not my fault he wasn't ready."

MUSTARD'S PICKLE

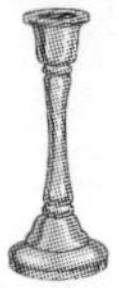

Colonel Michael Mustard sat at the long dining room table and stared at the gray lumpy substance in the bowl before him. Scottish oatmeal porridge, Mrs. White had said with some pride as she placed it on the mahogany table. Say what you will, he'd been served porridge before and it didn't look, or smell, anything like this. This had the consistency of mashed potatoes and the aroma of cloves. Reminded him of the time in India when the house servants had produced a faintly yellow breakfast dish that sent his mother racing for the facilities.

Perhaps a simple meal of toast and jam would be best to prepare him for the trials this day would bring. Simplicity and plain food had served him well in the barracks in South Africa. Nothing like a utilitarian early morning breakfast to set a man up for the day when he had an unpleasant chore on his roster.

However, the porridge must be dealt with. He tiptoed down the passageway with his bowl, slipped out the front door, and found a hidden spot to dump it under a rhododendron.

On his return to the dining room, he ducked his head into the kitchen. "What ho, Mrs. White. Might I have some toast?"

"Porridge not suit you?"

"The porridge was excellent. I'm just a little ravenous this morning after my walk around the grounds."

"If it's not one thing it's another." Mrs. White stopped whacking a paper bag with a lead pipe. "I'll not get the coffee ground in time for elevenses. I suppose you want fried eggs and blood pudding with the toast."

"Simply toast will do, six slices if you would be so kind."

She sighed and dropped six slices of bread on the hot surface of the Aga cooker. When they curled at the edges, she turned them over and pressed them flat. A moment later she shoveled them onto a plate and handed it to him. "The butter's on the table. Jam, too, made from the raspberries grown right here in the garden."

"Thank you. That will be sufficient." He returned to the dining room and tucked in with relish, slathering the hard dry toast with butter but ignoring the bowl of pink sticky froth Mrs. White called homemade red raspberry jam. Plenty of tea to wash it down, and he would be comfortably, and safely, full. He had no time to spare for an upset constitution.

Mrs. White had stationed the place settings a sword's length apart down the twenty-foot table. Gave him plenty of legroom. By the looks of it, only one other person had been in for breakfast so far, leaving a trail of crumbs and a tea stain on the once-white tablecloth. Apparently laundry was not Mrs. White's strong suit. The sun flooding in the tall windows was not kind to the damask's faults.

He was willing to wager the other early riser was not that empty-headed Miss Scarlet. Young people these days, no sense of duty or manners. Miss Scarlet proved a lazy stay-a-bed, although a shining example of feminine pulchritude.

His breakfast finished, he swept the loose crumbs from the tablecloth into his hand and deposited them on his plate. Plate and cup he aligned squarely at his place, with knife in the four o'clock position on the plate. A place for everything and everything in its place. On second thought, he dipped the knife in the jam and smeared it on the blade. It was always prudent to stay on the right side of the cook. He repositioned the knife.

Now, on to face the day, and the unpleasant task on his roster. His publisher had sent another threatening letter. *Produce your memoirs immediately.* He supposed this would be a bad time to ask for another advance. He'd have to write a second chapter first.

So, chop-chop, tally-ho, onward up the hill. He'd find out from that Professor Plum fellow how to go about writing a book. He'd heard Plum had penned a fine treatise on the dynasties of ancient Egypt while he'd been in the employ of the British Museum. Surely the man must know a thing or two about authoring. Might help him along, even write a chapter as demonstration.

He found Professor Plum pottering about in the library, poking the bookcases, prodding the ancestral portraits, fingering the hanging displays of weaponry. "See here, Plum, bit of a sticky wicket. Need a word or two with you about writing. Working on my memoirs, you see. Publisher getting fidgety, you know how they are, no patience for the creativity involved."

Plum blinked once or twice. "Yes, no, ah yes, I see, don't think I can be of much help. Sorry." He turned back toward the bookcases. "Odd kind of library, this, with the books locked up in cabinets."

"Thievery, my dear boy, one cannot be too careful. Sir Hugh never did trust the common folk. Liked to keep his books shipshape and Bristol fashion. Nicely done, I must say, all the red covers together, all the blue covers in another case. Can't allow the rank and file to muck about with them. Next thing you know there'd be anarchy."

Professor Plum cast a startled eye over the four bookcases, meshed doors locked. "By Jove, you're right. I hadn't noticed. Blue in this cabinet, red in that, green near the window, gray over there."

"Of course I'm right. Don't win battles by being wrong. Attention to detail, my dear boy. That's what wins the war. I dare say some of these books are collectables, some antiques, some just rubbish, but they look the part and fill the shelves. Sir Hugh was protecting them. Discouraging the riff raff from settling into the window seat with coffee and a book, licking the corners, bending the spine, smudging the pages with chocolate, that sort of thing."

"Yes, I see. We should read the newspapers instead. I think they are delivered every morning." He gestured to the library tables, spread with several days' issues of the leading dailies, plus a sampling of tabloids.

"Quite so. I dare say John Boddy is equally concerned about protecting this collection, since it will all be legally his in a fortnight." He stepped to the closest cabinet and tapped the lock with his riding crop. It fell open. "Perhaps not. Boddy must not be a book man. But back to the task at hand. Need a bit of guidance in the writing of the memoirs. Wondered if you could be of assistance. I could dictate, and you could write. I am reminded of the time my battalion was holed up in the Sudan."

Professor Plum snatched a book from the open cabinet and fled the room.

Undeterred, Colonel Mustard pressed on. When a battle plan proves faulty, regroup and take the next logical step.

He marched to the conservatory to take some fresh air, clear his mind. A brisk tour of the fish tanks to liven the heart, the scent of geraniums to tone the brain, the sound of water trickling down the fountain to, well, never mind.

Somewhere in the house he heard the echo of a shrill voice. “You can’t show that to anyone! I’ll be ruined! Again!” The voice was so high pitched it was unrecognizable as male or female.

A short silence followed, broken by a muffled report. Reminded him of the battlefield in South Africa, when he’d been poring over charts in the command post while the others in his regiment went toe to toe with the enemy. Clearly other guests had risen from their beds and fought to the death with the porridge.

If he cleared his mind of intrusions, he’d be able to formulate a plan of attack for the memoirs. He amused himself by reading a tabloid left on the chaise lounge until he heard a welcome sound, the gong announcing morning coffee was served in the lounge.

Apparently those who could not locate the breakfast table at a decent hour had no trouble wafting into the lounge at eleven. Mrs. Peacock, her hair marcelled under a flowered headband, lolled over the best chintz chesterfield, delft cup in hand, with a wedge of Dundee cake balanced on the saucer.

“Good morning, Colonel, just getting up?”

“Morning? I’ve been up since dawn, dear lady. The best part of the day is gone.” He helped himself to coffee and settled into the green leather easy chair. “I’ve been seeking assistance about writing my memoirs. Plum isn’t any help. Know of anyone?”

“You ought to ask John Boddy, his father was a journalist.”

“You ought to ask Miss Scarlet, she’s been in the papers enough,” Mr. Green said from the doorway. “She’d know something about the writing of exploits. Are there any cakes to go with that coffee?”

“What do I know about the writing of exploits?” Miss Scarlet asked as she entered the room in a long Chinese silk kimono, her hair askew.

Colonel Mustard stood, bowed slightly in her direction and retired from the room. It was far too early to listen to her prattle. One would think swanning around a Hollywood movie set was more important than the Boer War. He'd repair to the library and devise a strategy for writing the memoirs. There might be a pen and paper in one of the drawers.

There was no peace in the library, however. Mr. Boddy sprawled on the copper oval rug, a bullet hole in his chest. A gentle nudge with a riding crop, to check for vital signs, sent flakes of burned paper fluttering in the air around him

Take charge, take charge. Military training stood one in good stead in times of crisis. Secure the perimeter.

Obviously, Boddy had been shot. First step, then, examine the weaponry at hand. He sniffed the barrels of the row of pistols, revolvers and rifles hung on the wall. Yes, this .38 Special revolver had been recently fired. Interesting.

Next he examined the paper fragments. Printed material, not hand written, so it must be from a book or newspaper. Either Boddy held it in front of him, or the assailant held it in front of or over the revolver to deaden the sound or hide the weapon. Mixed with the paper were scraps of red cloth. Must be the cover of a book. That eliminated the newspapers scattered around the tables. There were no red books on the tables.

Where would one hide a book with a bullet hole in it? With other books, of course. He scanned the bookshelves. None were out of color alignment. One red book, however, stood out of height alignment. He pulled it out. A gaping hole through the middle rendered it unreadable, but he could make out most of the title and half the author's name.

He returned to the lounge, where everyone clotted around the coffee and cream. He strode in with more drama than a certain failed actress had in her pinky finger, and leveled an accusing riding crop at his suspect. “I accuse you of shooting Mr. Boddy with the revolver in the library.”

Mustard's Pickle

Solution:

The entire group hurried to the library after him.

Professor Plum snatched a long barreled gun from the display. "Stand back, all of you. I'm warning you. One step and you're goners."

"I don't think so, with that weapon, dear boy."

"That revolver was loaded. What makes you think this one isn't?" Plum blurted.

"That's a blunderbuss, my boy. Hasn't been used in a dog's age. All the accuracy of a heaved watermelon. John Boddy wasn't running an arsenal. He merely loaded one or two weapons in case of attack. A sound battle plan. I suspect, however, that this one is loaded." Colonel Mustard plucked a pistol from a wall mount. "This is a Colt .45, and quite accurate at close range." He leveled it at Professor Plum. "I am an excellent shot, too."

Plum lowered his weapon in defeat. "I surrender," he said.

"Why did you do it, old chap?"

"Boddy had a copy of my book, and he had found out where I got it. He was going to expose me. Humiliate me once again."

"Is it that badly written?"

"No, it's quite good, actually. Only I didn't write it. A colleague did, but he came to an unfortunate end, and I thought, since his book was almost all written, and it was no use to him, well, what harm could be done?"

Colonel Mustard smiled. Plagiarism. No wonder the old chap couldn't be of any help with the memoirs. But what a capital idea. Find a memoir of similar heroism, change the dates, the names, adjust the events, and Bob's your uncle, a manuscript. He knew just the place to find the raw material, too. Unread books. Perhaps a blue one, or a red one, or even one of those gray ones.

SCARLET IN THE ABSTRACT

Miss Josephine Scarlet arrived at the lounge at ten-forty-five for her nine-thirty meeting with Mr. John Boddy. She paused to make a dramatic entrance, sweeping the double doors open and pausing, framed in dark oak. Mr. Boddy would make a nice change from those old doddery fellows she'd been dating, and he'd be inheriting Sir Hugh Black's fortune in another two weeks. He was a bit standoffish, but much could be forgiven with diamonds.

The lounge appeared empty. No, there was Mrs. Peacock, swanning around in an ice blue chiffon dress and turquoise hat, fussing with the green velvet drapes.

"Good morning, Mother."

"Oh, hello, Josephine. You're up early. Not early enough for breakfast, though, and I'm sure it's cleared away by now. Look at this velvet. It's probably been here since Queen Anne. I can't imagine who updates the decorating here. Putting those paintings in the same room as these drapes. There ought to be a law against it."

Miss Scarlet arranged herself on the chintz chesterfield facing the door. If she couldn't make an entrance, she could make an impression. "I'm meeting Mr. Boddy here this morning to take a tour of his art collection. Maybe he'll explain. Do you think these pearls look all right with this dress?"

"I think that maroon floral print looks hideous on you. The pearls are inconsequential. But look at these paintings. Boddy has a lot of explaining to do. Who'd put Picassos in with this decorating scheme? This is Refined Country House style, not Art Without Rules. The ceilings are high and the walls pale. They can't carry off the abstracts. We'll have to see about moving them. We can't enjoy our summer here with these atrocities. I can barely stand to stay in the same room with them. It's all very well to update the place with a new artist, one does get tired of ancestral portraits and pastoral scenes, but really, one must exercise caution. Just because Boddy lives here doesn't mean he can run the place to ruin. Not until his birthday, anyway."

"Are these Picassos?"

"Certainly they are, dear. If you'd stayed in school longer, you'd know these things. All boxes and triangles and indistinguishable subject matter. Cubist, they call it. Who else?" Mrs. Peacock tapped a gilt frame, knocking off a pushpin. "I could tell you a thing or two about art, if you cared to learn."

"No, thank you." She shuddered at the thought of spending from now until noon following the blue chiffon haze from room to room, unmasking decorating faux pas. "I'll wait for Mr. Boddy. He promised to tell me all about his house and his collection. And anyway, I happen to like those Picubists."

"Picasso and cubist. How long have you been an art aficionado? Fifteen minutes?"

"I don't fish at all, Mother. I'm fond of art. I have been since Miss Puce took us on a school tour of the Taint Gallery."

"That's 'Tate,' and I suspect you skipped away to shop."

Miss Scarlet frowned. How did her mother know these things?

A clatter and shriek echoed through the room. Miss Scarlet stood up. "I wonder what that is? Mr. Boddy must have dropped a painting. I think I'll go and look."

"Yes, do. And tell him if the Picassos are intended as an upgrade to the scheme, it isn't working. Nor is this aquamarine cushion. It matches neither the drapes nor the seating."

Miss Scarlet left the room. Anything to avoid listening to Mother carping about the placement of plaid with print.

She found the cause of the commotion in the entrance hall. Mrs. White stood in a circle of dropped groceries, tins of tuna rolling in every direction, clanking against the toes of the armor, hacking the legs of the Louis Quatorze table. Her hands clutched at her collar and her eyes were saucers of dismay. She was a finicky woman. She might not like her tuna shaken and stirred.

At Mrs. White's feet, the inert form of Mr. Boddy lay face down on the hardwood. Clearly he had been on his way to meet Miss Scarlet in the lounge, as he had dropped an art book. It must have been intended as a gift. She hoped it was an expensive book. She picked it up and surreptitiously searched for the price tag.

The Mr. Green knelt beside their host, taking a pulse, oblivious of his kelly green silk suit trousers coming in contact with floor grit. "I'm sorry," he said, "but he's dead. Gone to meet his Maker. Gone to that great mansion in the sky, hallelujah." He leaned back on his heels and picked up his rolled-up newspaper, tucking it under his arm. "We should call the doctor. Heart attack, I expect. Gathered into the bosom of the Lord. Come along, Mrs. White. You'll know the family physician. Let me help you carry the lettuce. Salad for lunch, is it? And none of those rhubarb leaves this time?"

Miss Scarlet considered swooning, but reconsidered after reviewing the audience. She thought it was an odd kind of heart attack that showed up as a nasty gash on the back of the head. She had a sinking feeling this would make her predicament more difficult. If only Boddy had waited to die until he'd had a chance to marry her. On the other hand, he hadn't inherited the mansion yet, so she might work something in her favor. A protest of the will, and a demand for justice with a stamp of feet in red sequined shoes, perhaps. If that didn't work, a little forging of signatures on a fake wedding license. She had learned a few skills at Miss Puce's.

High heel shoes clicked into the hall behind her. "Mr. Boddy's dead, Mother," she said, without bothering to turn around. The heels continued their traverse of the hall until they were beside her.

"Dead? Oh my heavens." Mrs. Peacock fanned herself with a lilac hanky. "Such a young man. Such a hopeful beneficiary."

"Cute, too. In a non-royal-family kind of way."

"My dear. You've had a dreadful shock. Let me help you to the library. So calming in there." Professor Plum appeared, hovering at her elbow. "Mrs. White will make you a bracing cup of tea."

Miss Scarlet shook him off and redirected him to Mother. He didn't seem to know what to do about the change in helpless ladies other than carry on, steering the new elbow towards the library. Mother went willingly. She was never one to pass up an opportunity for pampering.

What now? Miss Puce's etiquette class hadn't covered what to do upon finding a corpse. She ought to cover Mr. Boddy up, like they always did in films. She looked around and didn't see a convenient white sheet. There wasn't even a rug to roll him in. He lay on the clean shiny floor. The cleanliness was marred only by a crumpled bit of newspaper and a penknife under his hand. Looked like a good one, too. Ivory handle. She slipped it into her pocket.

Boots marched into the room behind her. "What ho, keep the area clear, keep the area clear." Colonel Mustard boomed at her, his epaulets twitching with authority. "Stand clear, Miss, stand clear."

Someone must have alerted the colonel. Miss Scarlet withdrew to stand under the door arch, in case anyone was watching. An actress should stand framed, when possible, and attempt to be the sole attraction in the frame. She noticed Mr. Boddy had a couple of staples stuck in the soles of his shoes, as if he had walked through the secretarial pool on a bad day.

Colonel Mustard shooed her right out of the hall, and stationed himself at the door like a good soldier. She stood near the staircase, wondering where to go next. She had a clear view of Mr. Boddy, lying on the shiny floor, legs in a tangle, and noticed some streaks leading to him from the study door. It appeared as if someone in dress shoes had dragged his feet on his way to the front door. That tedious Mrs. White would be livid. She was always going on about grass clippings and gravel chips.

Better mention it to her, so she could buff the floor before the police arrived.

Miss Scarlet strolled to the kitchen, stopping now and then along the passageway to admire a painting. Too bad she wouldn't get that art tour. There seemed to be some important paintings here. Some pretty ones, too. Not like those weird Picasso things in the lounge. Maybe someone else would explain them to her. As a last resort, she could look them up in her new art book. If it had lots of pictures.

In the kitchen, Mrs. White flapped around muttering while Mr. Green calmly helped himself to tea and shortbread cookies.

"What will become of the house now," she demanded of the biscuit tins as she jammed them in the cupboard. "Who'll pay the upkeep? Who'll invite the guests? We'll fall into ruin, within six months, sure enough. My sisters will have to take me in."

"I'm sure your situation won't be all that desperate," Mr. Green said. "Is there any cream? Perhaps you'd feel a little calmer if you did something routine. Like making a mutton pie for lunch." He waved around his rolled-up newspaper like a conductor.

"Cook? How can I cook with an oven in that state? Opened it this morning and there it was, all hot and smelly. Something awful has spilled. It's a wonder it didn't catch fire and burn the house down, right enough. And me with a new recipe to try from Mrs. Beeton's cookery book."

Miss Scarlet opened the Aga cooker's oven door. It was still quite warm and smelled very odd, a warm sweet chemical smell. There seemed to be a smear of something sticky on the racks, too. She nudged at it with a cautious finger. Yellow.

"Yes, I see what you mean," she said. "The oven is quite unusable. Perhaps you should fry fish cakes instead."

"Good idea," Mr. Green said. "Once that's done you could wipe out the oven and bake lemon tarts."

Mrs. White mumbled something and turned her attention to tossing lettuce and tomatoes together with fury. Helping herself to a cup of tea, Miss Scarlet left in search of more sociable companions.

Mrs. Peacock and Professor Plum lingered in the library. Mrs. Peacock was ensconced in a gray wingback chair and Plum tapped a footstool into place under her feet.

As she entered, the Professor swooped on her and claimed her tea. "I see you've brought a little sustenance for our Mrs. Peacock. She's had such a fright. Here, my dear, try this, it will perk you right up."

"Indeed, Professor. I feel much better. It's so restful in here, as you said. All the dark wood panels and soothing paintings. That's a Gainsborough, I believe, and that's a Monet."

"How can you tell?" Miss Scarlet asked.

"Style, tone, subject matter, composition. Each painter has his own. Really, Josephine, the things you don't know."

"And a little plaque on the frame stating title and artist. That's always a give-away," Professor Plum added.

Miss Scarlet strolled around the library, examining the paintings. Each by a different artist, each with a different style. She carried on into the passageway, reading the plaques and flipping through her book to find them. This Picasso, he had the strangest style. People split in two, shattered colors. They looked like migraine headaches.

There were several Picassos in the study. Blotchy colors. Shaky lines. Looked like a bad attempt at crayoning done by a small child. Not what she'd care to hang in her home, if she had one. Over in the corner of the room she caught a whiff of that same smell from the oven, warm and sweet, comforting as if familiar. She couldn't place it. Nor could she find where it came from, although she bent down and sniffed the electrical outlets.

The gong rang for lunch. She joined the others in the dining room, the five of them spaced evenly down the twenty-foot table like gargoyles. A flustered Mrs. White served them a lettuce and tomato salad with dry tuna sandwiches. Nothing from the oven.

"Dreadful affair, this," Colonel Mustard said. "Boddy kicking off like that. Still, must carry on. I remember when I was stationed in the Sudan, and the General came a cropper."

He droned on for a while. Miss Scarlet tried to ignore him. She considered the others in turn. Mrs. Peacock disparaged the lack of any effort in the sandwiches other than taking the lid off the tin and dumping the contents on the bread. Mr. Green gorged himself on tomato wedges, his fingernails glowing greenly through the dripping juice. Professor Plum wore a distracted expression and fiddled with his bow tie. The Colonel kept talking, slapping the table with his riding crop now and then for emphasis.

"I say," Plum said, when Mustard had run out, "do you think we shall all be allowed to stay on, now that Mr. Boddy's gone? I'm at loose ends at the moment, and Green here is up against a knotty point."

Mr. Green flushed chartreuse. "I am not. My finances are in sound shape."

"Leave here? But we just arrived. That's hardly a holiday, is it?" Mrs. Peacock complained. "My daughter and I have come for the summer and we intend to stay. Don't we, Josephine dear?"

"Yes, Mother. Unless, of course, Noel Coward rings through to say he's got a part for me in his next play."

Mrs. Peacock fell into a fit of coughing.

Mrs. White returned from the kitchen with a fresh pile of sandwiches.

"Mrs. White, I found this candlestick on the floor in the study when I went to telephone the authorities," Colonel Mustard said. "It's got a bit of a red smudge on the base, and a green smear on the stem. I expect you'll want to clean it up. Can't have the house run to ruin, can we? Got to keep things shipshape."

"What do you all think of the paintings in the lounge?" Miss Scarlet asked. "Do you like those Cubist portraits?

"Excellent examples of Picasso's best, in my opinion," Professor Plum said. "A sight better than those in the study. Shoddy work there. Odd crinkle in the paint, too, as if it's older than it should be."

"What do you mean, crinkle?"

"You'll note if you study the ancestral portraits that the older they are, the more cracked the paint is. It happens, over fifty or a hundred years. Picasso is popular right now. I dare say the man is cranking them out as fast as he can. At any rate, the paint has hardly had a chance to dry, let alone crack, before he's sold it."

After a valiant attempt to eat an entire sandwich, Miss Scarlet excused herself. She wandered into the study with her art book and Professor Plum's assessment. In her book she found a photograph of one of the paintings. The real thing looked less polished than the photograph. The real thing had unsteady lines, and zigged where it should have zagged. She sat back in a chair beside the fireplace to consider this fact. She smelled that funny smell again. If the electric wiring were smoldering, they'd all be without a roof over their heads soon. Leaving her book on the table, she followed her nose to a bookcase and tugged at one of the unbooklike books. The wall creaked and swung open.

Ah-ha. A secret passage. Dark and musty and smelling strongly of the funny chemical scent. She inched down the staircase to the cold stone floor. There would be a wine cellar along here somewhere. She might just pick a good vintage for dinner. Mr. Boddy couldn't refuse to serve the best wines now, could he?

She found a light switch, and flicked it. A few dim recessed lights glowed. Well, it was better than nothing. She carried on her search, under cobwebs, past a fork in the passage and toward a distant narrow staircase. Yes, here was a wine cellar off the main passage, vaulted stone ceilings and old black wooden racks, and the funny smell again, more pungent now. The closest wine racks held lengths of canvas, rolls of tracing paper, and folded newspapers. There were bottles and tubes scattered around a worktable. Linseed oil and turpentine according to the labels, their lids not on tight. They were the source of the smell.

So the house wasn't burning down after all.

Ahead she could see the passage led to another set of stairs. She assumed they ascended to the kitchen, where one would go once one had selected a vintage. She browsed along the dusty racks until she found a bottle with a familiar label. Tucking it under her arm, she moved in the direction of the kitchen.

The lights went out.

She heard footsteps on the stone.

She scurried to where the stairs ought to be, her high heels clicking on the stones. The footsteps hurried after her, getting closer. A hand swiped at her. She felt the fingers grasp at her hair and miss.

Should she stop and clobber her adversary with the wine bottle? It would be a shame to waste such a fine vintage. She was almost at the stairs. She'd run faster. In a moment she'd be in the light of the kitchen.

Half way up the stairs a hand grabbed her ankle and yanked her down. Her stockings scraped on the wood, popped into holes, and she felt the ladders climb up from her shins.

The hands were pulling her down into the cellar. If only she had a weapon.

Why yes, the ivory handled penknife.

She snatched it from her pocket and stabbed at the hands.

Direct hit. Someone howled and let go.

She raced back up the stairs and burst into the kitchen.

Mrs. White glanced up from the cookery book. "Guests are not allowed in the wine cellar. You'll have to go back the way you came, Miss Scarlet. I can't have you traipsing into the kitchen through the secret entrance. It isn't done."

Miss Scarlet ignored her. She whirled around to her assailant, pointing the bottle of wine. "I accuse you of murdering Mr. Boddy in the study with the candlestick," she announced.

Scarlet in the Abstract

Solution:

Mr. Green fell out of the secret passage licking the small cut on his hand. "I didn't do it. I can explain."

"Good. Start by explaining why the Picassos in the study look funny. And why all that oil painting stuff is hiding in the wine cellar."

"I think John Boddy like to paint."

"If he does, he's not very good at it. Why would he trace the Picassos? I found pushpins in the frames and tracing paper. Why would he copy paintings he already owns?"

"He was fond of them?"

"That's silly. I know it was you. You have paint under your fingernails. And you had some on your hands which got smeared on the candlestick."

Mr. Green slumped against the wall and stared at his incriminating fingernails. "It was working so well. I was taking the real paintings away rolled up in newspaper, creating substitutes, and putting them in the empty frames after I had aged them. Could I have my penknife back?"

"Professor Plum said the Picassos shouldn't be aged."

"I wish I had known that. It would have saved me time, and we might have gotten a lemon tart for lunch."

"Why did you copy those weird Picasso things? Why not some of the nicer works?" Miss Scarlet wished she had her art book handy. She'd show him which paintings she'd like copied.

"I picked them because they were easy to copy, not like those paintings with people's faces."

"Why did you go to so much trouble? Are you broke? Are you selling them on the private market?"

"No, I'm not broke, just suffering a cash-flow problem. It will all be righted soon. My private collectors don't ask questions when they buy a painting. I thought John Boddy would be happy holding imitations with authenticated provenance. He doesn't have many guests. No one would notice."

"But John found out?"

"I'm afraid John caught me red-handed stapling an imitation into a frame."

"So you coshed him with a candlestick in the study. Then you dragged him toward the front door!"

"Yes, I thought he'd be better off in the garden. Mrs. White wouldn't have to deal with strangers cluttering up the study. I had to abandon that plan when she came in the door. I just needed a little money to tide me over, just several thousand pounds."

"You'll need more than that," Miss Scarlet said. "You owe me a new pair of stockings."

To Be Continued

"If I might be so bold as to inquire, Mrs. White, what is this?" Colonel Mustard indicated his plate, upon which resided a piece of stiff toast, topped by oozing stewed tomatoes, a scattering of limp cheese, and a peculiar orange-tinged mushroom. Against the backdrop of the white damask tablecloth, it looked surreal, a soft stack of ruby, alabaster and burnished gold.

"That's your breakfast, that's what that is."

"Yes, I understand the timing of the presentation. But what would be the name of this culinary triumph?"

Mrs. White smiled. "It's a new recipe that Mrs. Peacock gave me. She's a one for fancy cooking, is our Mrs. Peacock. Don't think she does any of it herself, but she likes a change from the regular fry-up. Anyroad, she gave me this recipe she brought back from France or Italy or one of them countries. Quiche Lorraine, she called it."

Colonel Mustard stared at his plate. "I've had Quiche Lorraine before, on a tour of duty in Tunisia. Might I suggest this doesn't resemble the dish as I recall it."

"Oh, well, I had to make a couple of substitutions, didn't I? The recipe started with pastry. I don't have time to fuss with pastry at this hour of the morning, so I used the toast left over from yesterday's breakfast.

Waste not, want not, you know. The filling called for a mix of eggs, bacon, onion, cream, and three kinds of cheese. That sounded like yesterday's bacon and eggs, and what's the point in trying something new if it's the same as you've been having, so I opened up a tin of stewed tomatoes instead. They wanted three fancy cheeses grated and mixed in with the cream to blend. I only had cheddar, which I grated as instructed, but there didn't seem much point in creaming it, since it was just the one kind. It looked a little plain when I was done, so I put a mushroom on it for fancy. And Bob's your uncle, Quiche Lorraine. Wasn't nearly as difficult as I thought it would be. I guess this foreign cooking is a bit of all right."

"Where did you get the mushroom?"

"Down at the end of the garden, a nice big fat one just growing there on the edge of the woods."

One thing a man learns, in twenty-seven years of military service, is never eat an unidentified wild mushroom. He'd seen men keel over into their bacon, eggs and fried mushrooms. "I wonder, Mrs. White, if you'd have one without the mushroom. My digestion is a little touchy by times."

"I do. I made such a batch of these, and there was only one mushroom."

He leaned away from his plate. "Then I shall have one without the mushroom."

Mrs. White's black and white uniform crackled as she removed the quiche, but she brought him a replacement and refilled his teacup with restored grace.

As he worked his way through the tasteless breakfast imposter, he mulled over his next move. Clearly, it was his duty to warn the others about the potential hazard decorating the breakfast special. Judging by the undisturbed place settings spread around the long table, he was the first one up. No one else had as yet been introduced to the poisonous orange mushroom.

Should he march to their rooms, rouse them, warn them? Or should he lie in wait and ambush them with the information? A gentleman should not barge into a lady's boudoir unannounced and uninvited. He couldn't storm Mrs. Peacock's quarters. She would be mortified. Miss Scarlet was another matter entirely. She might think he was paying a social call.

Miss Scarlet. She of the pouting, whining conduct unbecoming to a lady. Why should he warn her?

And Green, sanctimonious preacher of the gospel, always spouting bits of scripture, a most annoying man. Why should he warn Green?

The dining room door opened and Professor Plum wandered in, a folded newspaper under one arm, his bow tie askew, a barely suppressed yawn on his lips. "Good morning, Mustard. What say you today? Do you happen to know if the Intelligence industry has need of a professor of antiquities?"

"Out of a job, are we?"

"Yes, since the British Museum cut back on staff, I find myself at loose ends. Ah, good morning, Mrs. White. Tea, please." He glanced down at his plate. "What is that yellow thing?"

"It's a new recipe Mrs. Peacock gave me. Quiche Lorraine."

"No, I mean the yellow thing. What is it?"

Colonel Mustard excused himself. Professor Plum could clearly handle his own defence. He carried his teacup down the passageway. He'd round out his breakfast hour with the day's paper in the lounge while he mulled over his plan of attack for the other guests.

A sudden through struck him as he settled into the green leather easy chair in the lounge. Would John Boddy be sufficiently aware of Mrs. White's culinary foraging that he would be wary of a yellow tidbit at breakfast? It didn't do to leave some things to chance. Boddy held the purse strings, and delightfully weighty strings they were. He couldn't in good conscience allow Boddy to succumb to a malicious mushroom. This was a time for action.

There was a light on in Boddy's study. Either he had worked late or he had risen early. Colonel Mustard approached the partially open door and rapped smartly with his riding crop. He received no response. He repeated the rap. Still no response.

"I say, Boddy," he said, boldly striding into the study, "bit of a sticky wicket in the dining room."

He stopped dead at the center of the maroon rug. John Boddy was slumped in his red leather desk chair, his face on his papers and a knife in his back.

The colonel stepped up and tested the body for vital signs by giving it a poke with his riding crop. Eliciting no response, he reached for the telephone. A quick call to the local constabulary, and this matter would be in the hands of the authorities. Each man to his own job, and they were the fellows to solve murders. He could then carry on his previous mission, to warn or not warn the others about the mushroom.

He glanced over the oak roll-top desk as he placed the call. Boddy had been working on something involving a lot of money, judging by the figures scribbled in the margins of the pages. Using his riding crop, he slid the top page out from under Boddy's head. *Party Planning.* Quite so. Boddy's thirtieth birthday was in a couple of weeks. No doubt he planned to invite the neighbors to a little soirée.

More than just the neighbors, by the looks of the guest list. My, my, this was interesting. A soldier who had once served as a warrant officer ought to take charge of this project. Just because a man was dead was no reason to cancel a large important social gathering. There were names here that would be useful should the settlement of Sir Hugh's estate lean to the unfavorable.

Colonel Mustard collected all the necessary papers from the desk. He moved Boddy's knees so he could search the desk drawers for catalogues, brochures, and letters. When he was satisfied he had all the necessary materials, he rearranged the body in its original position.

What an armload of papers. It would take him all day to work through them. He'd need a command post for this operation. An area with adequate square footage for the proper alignment of papers and files. The dining room would be ideal. The table was at least twenty feet long, with the six place settings spaced evenly around it. They could be grouped at one end, leaving the rest of the table for his important work.

As an added bonus, he'd be on site to warn the others about the toxic fungus à la carte.

Without further ado, he betook his booty to the dining room and established himself at one end of the table. He only needed to move two place settings closer together to secure nine uninterrupted feet of empty table space. He began sorting his papers in order of urgency.

Miss Scarlet appeared at the dining room door, draped in a cerise satin dressing gown. She groped her way to the teapot with eyes half closed. Really, a proper young lady would complete her toilette before arriving at the breakfast table. It was bad form to display one's nightwear to the gentlemen of the house. She seemed unaware of his presence as she sat down at her place, pushed her place setting away, and laid her head on the damask.

"Sit up, Josephine," Mrs. Peacock's voice rang in the room and jangled the chandelier. The feathers on her robin's egg blue hat waggled in indignation.

"Mother, don't shout. I've such a head this morning."

"Nothing that a little food in your stomach wouldn't cure. Oh, good morning, Colonel."

"Good morning, madam. If I might have a word with you—"

"Not now, Mustard. I'd like my breakfast first. I asked Mrs. White to make—"

"Quiche Lorraine. And here it is." Mrs. White marched in with a tray of the delicacy of the day.

"That's not Quiche Lorraine."

"Yes it is. I followed the recipe. What's happened to the place settings? What are you doing with all those papers on my table?"

"Quiche Lorraine is based on pastry. I don't see any pastry here." Mrs. Peacock pointed at the toast. "And what's this awful yellow thingy?"

"Why can't we have coffee at breakfast?" Miss Scarlet asked, her voice muffled by her satin elbows.

"Just setting up a command post to run the party." Colonel Mustard spoke up before Mrs. Peacock worked herself up over the quiche.

"It's a mushroom," Mrs. White said. "Coffee belongs at elevenses, not before. Party? There won't be any birthday party. Master John is dead. I'll not have you messing up my table. The place settings are spaced correctly. You can't go pushing them together like that."

"Dead? John's dead?" Miss Scarlet lifted her head from the table.

"Yes. Afraid so. Sticky wicket. But I'm taking charge of the birthday party he was organizing. Nothing a logistics expert like myself can't handle smoothly. We'll have to change the name, call it a memorial party or something, but the show must go on." Colonel Mustard tapped the table with his riding crop. "The guest list includes His Royal Highness Edward the Prince of Wales. Known to his family as David."

"David? David's coming to the birthday party? Mother, I must have a new dress. I cannot have him see me in something tatty. We'll have to go to London."

"This in no way resembles Quiche Lorraine. I am completely disappointed. I refuse to eat this. Get me some plain toast."

"Well, I never, after all the trouble I went to, and the Colonel liked it just fine, didn't you, Colonel? But you can take all that paper off my dining table. A dining table is for dining, not writing. If it were for writing, they'd have called it a writing table. Honestly, I'll have to reset the places you moved. As if I don't have enough to do already, what with people changing their minds about breakfast and ordering toast."

Mrs. White pushed his papers onto his knees, and it was all he could do to contain the fallout. He fumbled everything into a heap and left the dining room. Mission Two was in disarray. However, Mission One was accomplished with ease. Mrs. Peacock had refused the mushroom. Miss Scarlet had refused food. Mr. Green could receive his warning from a Higher Power. His work here was done.

The library looked like a suitable location for a logistics command post.

After clearing the newspapers off the largest table, he spread his papers out and began again. First, sort out the categories of tasks, then set up a priority list. That was the way to get things done in this man's army. Order and logic. Guest list, musicians, rations, flowers, decorations, birthday cake. Well, scrap that, or change it to memorial cake. No point in canceling an order for a triple-tiered chocolate cake if one didn't have to. Particularly after a fortnight of Mrs. White's cooking.

He spent a happy half-hour sorting and re-sorting papers. Sort by topic, re-sort alphabetically, and then re-sort by priority. Shuffle and move, change and rearrange. Lovely, lovely paperwork. The kind of thing that kept a man alive while all around him his colleagues were getting shot to bits on the battlefield.

Slowly a portrait of the proposed birthday party emerged from the separate sheets. An intimate dinner for fifty of Boddy's closest friends, followed by dancing in the ballroom to a live orchestra. The piping of the dignitaries to the stage at midnight. A ceremonial cake cutting. An official handing over of the keys to the mansion, and a red box representing the investment portion of the estate. Some speeches. HRH Edward the Prince of Wales would say a few words. As a grand finale, a speech by Boddy, thanking his friends for joining him on this auspicious evening.

Surely Boddy intended to say more that that. Where was the plan outlining the continued trust funds to those Sir Hugh had valued most?

Boddy had not finished the speech. That was the only possible reason for the omission. Just because the last line said 'Thank you all, and good night' did not mean the speech was complete.

Colonel Mustard was so engrossed in his work he didn't hear the gong for morning coffee. He did, however, notice the lead pipe that went whizzing past his ear and landed with a clonk on the far end of his table.

He ceased his musings and retrieved the pipe. That was most peculiar. How would a lead pipe come to be sailing through the air? He could have been injured, or worse. Someone needed a sharp reprimand. He placed the pipe with his papers and peered up and down the passageway. It was empty, but laughter rippled from the lounge. He checked his watch.

In jig time he was comforting himself with hot coffee and a wedge of shortbread.

"What's all this about Boddy being dead and us carrying on with his birthday party?" Mr. Green asked. "It sounds like a good idea. Blessed are those who rejoice in the valley of the shadow."

"Is anyone missing a lead pipe?" the Colonel asked.

"It'll hardly be a birthday party if he's no longer entitled to birthdays," Professor Plum pointed out.

"But the Prince of Wales is invited, so we can't cancel," Miss Scarlet said.

"He's not invited yet." Mrs. White shook her head as she refilled the biscuit tray. "The invitations haven't been posted."

"Ah, good." Mustard said. "That gives me a little time to change the format. Reprint the invitations to reflect the change."

"Then that gives me time to go to London for a new dress. Mother, you can't possibly expect me to greet David in the same sequined gown I wore last time. You must have some money stashed away somewhere."

My, how that young woman could prattle on about trifles. Colonel Mustard tucked an extra shortbread in his pocket and returned to his library lair. This business about the invitations not being posted was troubling. Where were they if they hadn't been delivered? Surely Boddy would have posted them. One cannot secure the attendance of the Prince of Wales without giving him sufficient notice. He made a note to write fresh invitations.

Next in importance was booking a top-flight orchestra. Boddy had made a list and ticked off one group in particular, The Hampton Court Frolic and Frim-Fram.

Colonel Mustard moved to the telephone table beside the window and rang through to the number Boddy had scribbled beside the name. A laconic young woman's voice echoed down the line.

"The Hampton Court Musicians. How may I help you?"

"I should like to book the orchestra for the evening of June 17th, please. Tudor Hall, John Boddy."

"You were already booked for that night, sir."

"Excellent. Just verifying."

"But you cancelled."

"Cancelled?"

"Yes. The group has accepted another engagement in the meantime. Sorry."

"When was the booking cancelled?"

"I don't know. I only work here."

The telephone hummed in his ear.

This was a setback. He'd try the other groups on the list. After an hour on the telephone, he had learned that two groups were booked, one had disbanded, and one played the new music by Duke Ellington, and was he sure that's what he wanted? He most certainly did not. But don't give up the ship. In a pinch he could invite his Aunt Ida. She was a whiz on the piano.

While he was using the telephone, he'd call the greengrocer and see about the rations for the dinner.

"Smidgen and Snub."

"Good day to you, sir. I am calling regarding the upcoming dinner party at Tudor Hall. Do you have our order for two legs of lamb, a crown roast of pork, a hip of beef, fifty pounds of potatoes, forty pounds of carrots, a bushel of peas, and a pint of mint sauce?"

"No, sir, I do not. When is this party?"

"In twelve days time."

"I say, this is rather short notice for an order of this size. You should have placed it weeks ago."

"I see. Well, water under the bridge. Can you accommodate me?"

"I'll do my best. Read the list to me again so I can write it down."

A tedious ten minutes later, Mr. Smidgen seemed to catch the drift of it, and Colonel Mustard rang off.

Something flew past his ear. He heard a loud crash, and a fine white ash rained down on him. He leaped to his feet. A black and gold urn lay in shards around him, and the source of the breakage seemed to be a wrench. How would a wrench fly past him and hit an urn? He might have been conked on the head with it. What was all this gray powder? This was an outrage. And a mess. He hurried to find Mrs. White.

She was dusting in the billiard room, humming a little Scottish melody to herself. When she saw him, she screamed and dropped her duster.

"What ho, Mrs. White, I don't mean to alarm you, but there's been an odd kind of accident."

"Are you coming back from the dead, to haunt me?"

"No, I'm quite alive. I must look a fright, though, all covered in gray dust. Some kind of urn broke in the library. On a shelf near the window. Bit of a mess to clean up. You'll want to set to it right away."

Mrs. White smoothed her apron and sidled away from him. "Urn. By the window. Which one? There are several."

"Black and gold, I believe. Greek design. Or Egyptian."

"That would be Sir Hugh's father. They brought him back from Africa in that."

Colonel Mustard beat an immediate retreat to his boudoir to assess the damage and make necessary repairs.

A short time later he took charge of his library post again, feeling quite dandy in his Royal Hampshire Regiment dress uniform. It seemed a little snug around the waist. Eight years in the closet had tightened it up. Must be the humidity.

Now, where was he? Oh, yes, find the lost invitations, prepare new invitations, tuck them in the old envelopes so as not to lose the postage stamps, and telephone Aunt Ida. This last chore was best delayed. Aunt Ida was getting on, and one had to shout to make her understand.

That brought the venue to the fore. A reconnaissance mission might be in order at this point.

He marched down to the ballroom, the scene of the proposed party. The immaculate hardwood and gold brocade furnishings lent the proper tone for the party. The chandelier needed buffing, and he knew Mrs. White would be only too happy to oblige. He would even hold the ladder for her. The piano was already mounted on the small stage opposite the grand curved staircase, and chairs aligned for the orchestra. He'd have Mrs. White remove them, so there'd be room to gather around the piano.

The dancing would fill the entire room, but there should be chairs set around for the ladies to rest. Mrs. White could do that. She knew which chairs were moveable. The piping of the dignitaries to the stage would require a red carpet runner. He'd ask Mrs. White to look after that.

He ought to delegate a few tasks. Mrs. Peacock could act as official hostess. Mr. Green could say grace before dinner, if he could keep it under two minutes. Professor Plum could be assigned the cutting of the cake, if he promised to keep his fingers out of the icing while the speeches were going on. Miss Scarlet, well, there didn't seem to be a suitable job for an empty-headed starlet, other than clinging to the arm of the Prince of Wales.

The cake required a sturdy table. He climbed the steps onto the stage and strolled across the proscenium. He could establish the podium at center stage, with the piano off to the left and the cake equidistant to the right. HRH would not play second fiddle to chocolate.

A silver candlestick whizzed past his ear, punching a hole in the scenery panels.

He was so surprised he leaped toward the wings and fell into the red velvet curtains. A cloud of dust set him coughing, and he grasped for a handhold while he recovered himself. Really, how had a candlestick come to be flying through the air? He could have been clobbered in the head. He could have been killed, or injured, and how long would it be before anyone found him here on the ballroom stage? No one in the house came here to idle away their time. He could lie here for hours, the life seeping out of him, and nobody the wiser. This was untenable.

He rolled into a crouch and peeked around the curtains. The coast was clear. His shoulder brushed against something. A box, hidden behind the curtain. He pushed aside the velvet. Inside lay a pile of invitations, stamped and sealed.

Mystery solved. He peered around the curtain again. The ballroom was completely empty. He hoisted the box and hurried back to his library command post. There he poured the invitations on his table and placed the empty box on the floor at the three o'clock position. Shipshape.

Someone did not want these invitations mailed. No matter. That tardiness had worked in his favor. He would open the seal, cross out the word *Birthday*, replace it with *Memorial*, and congratulate himself on another task drawn to a successful conclusion.

As he sorted and stacked the prodigal invitations, he mulled over the planning. He'd never had so many problems with logistics. The orchestra cancelled, the invitations not sent, the food not ordered. He'd have to ring the florist next, and see if the order had been placed for thirty bouquets of roses and a dozen balloons. He had his suspicions.

A sharp boom echoed in his ear. He dived under the table and hugged the copper oval rug. That was a sound he knew all too well, the report from a revolver. The mirror opposite his chair shattered into a thousand shards that cascaded onto the hardwood.

He craned his head around while remaining cowered under the table. He could see the nose of a smoking gun poking through the keyhole. Someone definitely had dishonorable intentions.

"I accuse you of stabbing Mr. Boddy in the study with the knife," he shouted, hoping several people might overhear and run to his rescue.

To Be Continued

Solution:

The door swung open.

Mrs. White stood in the doorway with the revolver pointed at his head. "You're quite right. And you're next."

"But why?"

"It was all well and good, me living here looking after Master Boddy all these years, but as soon as his birthday pops up, he wants to invite you lot to stay for a few weeks. Such a load of work that's brought me. Cooking and cleaning up after, changing the beds, dusting the whatnots, I've not a moment to myself. Then he announces he's throwing a big birthday party. Inviting all the mucky-mucks. And who'll be cooking dinner for all those people, and seeing the ballroom is in perfect condition? Me, that's who. I cancelled the orchestra and didn't place all the orders, but when he handed me the box of invitations, I knew I had to do something. I had to stop that party or I'd be run right ragged."

The revolver wavered in her hand. Colonel Mustard remained under the table, clutching a chair leg for cover.

"But why me? Why shoot at me?"

"Because you're going on with it, aren't you? I killed him to stop the party and now I'll have to kill you."

Colonel Mustard crawled out from under the table, laughing a hearty forced laugh. "My dear Mrs. White, you had only to say the party was a difficulty and cancelled it is. Just like that. No more planning. No more work. Here, I'll shove this lot and we can forget we ever thought about it. How does that suit?"

The revolver drifted downward. "That sounds much better."

"Of course it does." With one hefty swipe in the three o'clock direction, he cleared the table of papers, and they fell into the empty box. "There, the party's finished. If you would direct me to the dustbin, I'll dispose of it. And then what say we have one of your lovely cups of tea? I've had a stressful morning, as I am sure you have also. A cup of tea will set us right. And one of your wonderful jam tarts with it, if you have any on hand. I don't mind waiting while you bake a few."

A Feather in Every Cap

Professor Plum took his morning coffee into the conservatory. A little basking in the sun would warm his spirits. My, that had to be the biggest aspidistra in the world. And that ivy, tendrils insinuating themselves all along the rafters and into every handy pot, becoming an uninvited flat-mate to unsuspecting hosts. How long could he insinuate himself into John Boddy's good graces? Bit of a tight spot, being dismissed from the British Museum. He needed to raise some cash to carry on the lifestyle to which he was accustomed. Sir Hugh had treated him well with the funding for his research in Egypt, but that might end in another two weeks, when Boddy turned thirty and took control of Sir Hugh's estate.

What would Mum Plum say? "Work, Peter, work." If she knew he was out on his ear, she'd rant at him about the waste of a fine mind, and the squandering of an expensive education.

He'd better find a job before Mum caught wind of his situation.

A jumble of newspapers lay on the garden bench. Another pile of them was wedged between the aspidistra and split-leaf philodendron pots. He could scan the advertisements, see if anyone wanted to hire an expert on ancient Mid-Eastern culture. A private collector, willing to send the right man on an archeological dig to Egypt, and interested in artifacts slipped quietly out of that country and into the personal collection.

Wanted—Specialist in Egyptian Antiquities. Apply British Museum.

Oh dear, that was his old job. He drew the papers from between the plant pots and flipped through the pages. *Russians Withdraw from War, Revolution on the Home Front.* What the devil? That sounded like the Great War. Ah. The paper was dated 1917. Apparently Mrs. White was not assiduous at clearing away the weeklies. This one had been stuffed between the pots for nine years.

He was about to jam the paper back in the crevice when his attention snagged on another headline. *Sir Matthew Peacock Dies in Boating Mishap.*

Well, well, well.

He settled on the bench to read.

Sir Matthew Peacock, noted London barrister, died today in a boating incident in the Lake District. Sir Matthew had been enjoying an early morning swim when friends suggested he try aqua-boarding. He was experiencing some measure of success when a rogue motorboat racing across the lake struck him, cutting the towrope and flinging him through the air. The unidentified driver, clad in a navy overcoat, failed to stop at the scene. The suspect motorboat was later found abandoned two miles along the shore. Sir Matthew's wife, Patricia Gobelin Scarlet Zaffer Peacock, was devastated by the news of her husband's untimely demise. Police had been delayed in locating her to inform her of the tragedy as she had been out on a long walk.

Very interesting indeed. There was something odd about this account, something puzzling. He did love puzzles. They were more fun than looking for a job. He'd have a go at this one.

Who would have been around when Sir Matthew died? Colonel Mustard had been going on and on about his exploits in military intelligence during the Great War. Perhaps he'd have an intelligent thing to say about the situation. Where would he be at this time of day? He had no idea what the other guests did all day. He'd have to ask Mrs. White.

Professor Plum cut through the ballroom on his way to the kitchen. Halfway across, his progress was halted by a shout from the top of the curved grand staircase. There followed a tumbling of arms and legs, and a scattering of papers. Plum leaped backward out of the way, threw himself off balance, and toppled into a heap.

When he reorganized himself, he found he was nose to nose with John Boddy. Mr. Boddy, however, was dead, while he, Plum, emerged uninjured except for a slight scrape to his pride. As there was no one to notice his predicament, the injury faded.

He rose, brushed off his tweeds, adjusted his bow tie, and surveyed the scene. Mr. Boddy had dropped some yellowed newspapers with holes cut in them. A quick scan revealed the years 1903, 1911, and 1917 on the newspaper banners. Stuck to Mr. Boddy's shoulder was a tiny cream-colored feather. Professor Plum lifted it off and tucked it in his waistcoat pocket. It seemed like a good idea, although he wasn't sure why. Maybe his collector's instinct. It might be the feather from a rare bird.

It seemed odd that Boddy would fall down his own stairs, as he had lived in this house since childhood. In all likelihood he was proficient at sliding down the banister. Professor Plum ascended the stairs part way, rounding the bend. At the top, he could see a rope tied from the base of one newel post to the opposite newel post. It seemed ideally situated to trip a fellow up at the ankles, if he failed to notice it. Or catch a fellow struggling to regain his balance after he'd been pushed. This was an altogether different puzzle.

Professor Plum returned to the bottom of the stairs. He ought to find Colonel Mustard and have him do something about Boddy. He would speak to Mrs. White, too. She'd know what to do.

He found the good lady in the kitchen plucking a chicken on the butcher's block table. The room danced in white feathers.

"I say, Mrs. White, have you seen the Colonel?"

"You might catch him at the front of the house, he was shooting in the woods at the end of the garden."

"Thank you. By the way, there's a bit of a problem to clean up in the ballroom."

"It will just have to wait, won't it? I've a chicken stew underway here." She held up the chicken by one leg. Most of it was plucked clean, while other spots bore tufts of down. "Close enough, I'll warrant," she said, dropping the bird in the stew pot.

"I say, aren't you going to clean out the innards?"

"Why? It's stew, isn't it? It's supposed to have lots of bits in it."

Plum withdrew, making a mental note to choose bread and butter for dinner. As he left, he noticed several chicken feathers clinging to his suit. He brushed them off, thought better of it, and saved a healthy specimen. He would compare it to the feather he had found on the body. But at the moment, he ought to find the colonel.

He found Mustard stomping his dirty boots through the front hall, a brace of pheasants on his arm, feathers fluttering.

"I say, do you have a moment, Colonel?"

"How do you like my catch, Plum? Potted the beggars right out of the rose gardens. That's the thing about a formal garden, it makes it dashed easy to retrieve your game if you haven't got a dog to do it for you." The colonel's face was flushed, as if he'd been hurrying.

"Excellent day's shooting. Do you perchance know how to pluck and clean them?"

"Indeed I do. A sportsman must know how to follow through. Why, I fed our regiment a few times when the supplies didn't come through and we were down to our last scoop of flour. I recall an evening in Tanganyika, when our tents were—"

"Could you do it today? Mrs. White seems not to have the finesse of it."

"Quite so. Delighted to oblige."

"As I was saying, I wonder if you remember the death of Sir Matthew Peacock, back in '17?"

"As clearly as this morning's prune custard. Bad business, that. We were all brought in from the field to help out. Connections at high levels, you know. Caused quite a stir in London. T'were no end of meetings and consternation. Tried to keep my involvement hush-hush, but you know the newspapers, always poking their noses in too far. Upshot of it was Sir Matthew's partners took over the firm and the widow retained his entire estate. He'd built it up to a hefty penny, too."

"Did you ever discover who did it?"

"No, never did. Found the motorboat the next day, of course, and a navy overcoat in the lake a few weeks later. I expect it was the work of a homicidal tramp. These things often are. Furor died down after a month or two. The partners got on with things and the widow learned to handle the affairs of the estate. Had some experience in that quarter, after Zaffer."

"Do you know anything about that?"

"You might ask Green. He's traveled in her circles by times." Colonel

Mustard shook the brace of pheasants. "Anything else? I need to get to work on these."

"No, no, carry on. Thank you for your time."

The colonel marched his muddy boots across the hall, scattering feathers with every step. Plum collected a tan one and added it to his pocket.

He found Mrs. Peacock playing solitaire in the lounge, while Miss Scarlet reclined on the chintz chesterfield with a book, looking bored and disheveled but insanely beautiful. She was wearing wide-bottomed vermilion trousers trimmed with pink ostrich feathers. Every time she sighed, another wisp of feather quivered away. Plum sidled along the back of the chesterfield and surreptitiously bagged a sample while breathing deeply of her perfume. Heady stuff.

"Has anyone seen Mr. Green?" he asked, feeling his puzzle getting fuzzy around the edges.

Miss Scarlet heaved a theatrical sigh. 'I'm sure I don't know where he is. I don't keep tabs on everyone. I have better things to do with my time." She waggled the book limply, sighed again, and resumed reading.

"How about you, Mrs. Peacock? Have you seen him?"

"I believe you'll find the Reverend in the library." She inclined her head to the door in question and a small blue feather drifted off her peacock-and-marabou turban.

"Thank you." Plum stumbled past her chair, and pretended his shoelace was undone so he could bend down and snag the feather.

Mr. Green was in the library shuffling around Sir Hugh's collection of stuffed birds of prey. He was holding a rather large specimen of a Great Gray owl when Plum entered.

"Good day, Plum," he said, dropping the owl back on the bookcase, causing a cascade of dust and feathers. "Praise be, Mrs. White will not be amused if she finds this mess." He made a show of sweeping the stray feathers under the copper oval rug. More danced along the fringe than disappeared. Plum helped himself to one for his collection.

"I was wondering, Reverend, if you knew Mrs. Peacock before she was Mrs. Peacock?"

"I remember her well. Mrs. Scarlet she was then. She was traveling in Italy, poor lonely young thing, and she met Ernest Zaffer. He was an ugly old coot, but he had a yacht and a highly placed circle of friends, and she fit right in. He sought me out and asked me if I'd marry them. I am a clergyman, as you know. It was a modest wedding, on the yacht with ice sculpted in the shape of sea birds and champagne flowing over ice-and-diamond fountains. Sadly, a year later he fell from their hotel balcony. I went to console the widow, naturally, but she'd already set sail in the yacht for England. Afraid I lost touch with her after that. You might ask Mrs. White. She's known Mrs. Peacock longer than the Israelites wandered the desert."

"Do you remember the year of that accident?"

"Certainly. As a man of the cloth I keep good records. Had to be, well, 1910. Or was it 1911? I think they were married in 1910, and he died a year later. It was in all the papers. Had a bit of a to-do with the press myself around that time and had to leave the country quickly."

"Thank you. You've been most helpful." Plum excused himself and left the library.

When he was alone along the passageway, he pulled all his feathers out of his pocket. If the person who pushed Boddy left the cream feather, he could match feathers and discover the perpetrator. Cream, white, gray, pink, tan, and blue. He tried to examine the form and structure of them, to identify species of origin. They all looked like feathers to him.

He arranged them in a row on his hanky and folded the lot into his pocket. Feathers were a more difficult puzzle than information. So far he had unearthed facts about 1917 and 1911, coinciding with the cut-up newspapers Boddy was carrying when he fell. He'd see what Mrs. White knew about 1903.

He found Mrs. White polishing the kitchen taps while a burning smell issued from the stew pot. "I say, Mrs. White, did you know Mrs. Peacock before she was Mrs. Peacock?"

"That woman. Miss Gobelin. Met her in 1900. Didn't I tell Mr. Boddy, as he was growing up, he was as close as two fleas from having her as a stepmother when he came to live here after his parents disappeared? Sir Hugh was mad about Miss Gobelin, he was, and she off and married James Scarlet. Sir Hugh was 36 at the time, must have seemed like an old gaffer to her at 23, and handsome James Scarlet more her age but not well off. Anyroad, Sir Hugh moped around for months afterward. Then didn't young James up and die a couple of years later. Left her a handsome insurance settlement and a little girl to raise. Sad, really. Poor lad fell down the stairs."

"That's a touching story, Mrs. White. Are you sure John Boddy would remember it? You told it to him as a child."

"He never tired of hearing it. Asked me to tell it to him again just last week. He seemed moved by it, too. Pretended to busy himself writing on his infernal papers, but I knew he was choking back a tear."

"Do you remember what year it was, when James Scarlet died?"

"Of course I do. 1903, it was. The same year that my Winslow died after dinner. It were his birthday, too, pour soul. I have the clippings from the newspaper."

Plum left the kitchen and paused in the empty dining room to review the facts of dates and persons. Like Mrs. White, John Boddy must have been collecting clippings from the newspapers. Someone had seen what he was up to, and arranged an accident while he was carrying the remains of the newspapers to the rubbish bin. That made sense, but he couldn't quite work the feathers into it.

Cream, white, gray, pink, tan, and blue.

Still, museums and collectors paid him to solve puzzles. He possessed the well-trained mind of a scholar and the deducting skills of an archeologist. Right. He'd use his brains, ingenuity and a little sleight of hand, one of the extra skills he'd learned working for Sir Hugh. Anyone would be pleased to hire him after they heard he'd solved this puzzle.

He returned to the lounge. Everyone was there now, Mrs. White cleaning windows and the other four playing Court Whist around a circular inlaid cherry table.

Professor Plum retrieved his hanky and unwrapped the feather collection. He was the only one who had seen the cream feather on Mr. Boddy's jacket. He pulled the blue feather from the group and held it high. "I found this blue feather on the body at the bottom of the stairs," he said, turning, "and I accuse you of killing Mr. Boddy in the ballroom with the assistance of a rope."

A Feather in Every Cap

Solution:

Mrs. Peacock shook her head. "Preposterous."

Miss Scarlet pointed at the turban. "Mother, you're molting. You're dropping feathers everywhere you go. Especially that white marabou down."

"I was in the ballroom and I examined the staircase." Colonel Mustard declared. "I found no rope."

"What's that, then?" Mrs. White said, pointing at a coil of something peeking out from under the cushion on Mrs. Peacock's chair.

"I did not tie a rope to the newel posts and push Boddy down the stairs," Mrs. Peacock stated. "Why would I do such a thing?"

Professor Plum took a long look at Mrs. Patricia Gobelin Scarlet Zaffer Peacock and her fondness for ropes and gentlemen falling.

Mr. Boddy had recently found out her secret, as evidenced by the newspaper clippings in his possession. Perhaps he had threatened to turn her in to the authorities. The next thing you know, he had fallen.

Now Plum himself knew the secret and was sharing a two-storey mansion with this woman. If she knew he knew, there'd be a rope taut at his ankle-height when he least expected it.

He shrugged. “I have absolutely no idea why you might do that.”

A Whiter Shade of Blue

"But you must know where they are, Mrs. White. You're in charge of décor." Mrs. Patricia Peacock waved a hand at the faded curtains and ancient floor tiles on the kitchen floor. Some people had no sense of the importance of keeping up appearances. "These were the paintings Sir Hugh and I collected in our short time together in 1901. Ah, the memories. Idyllic days." She dabbed an azure hanky at the corner of her eye. "Do you know, the last time I saw him in Paris, it was right before the War, he took me shopping and bought me the most divine powder blue Coco Chanel suit."

"I'm sure I don't know cocoa from chocolate when it comes to clothes, ma'am," Mrs. White said. "In Scotland we confine ourselves to sorting tartan from plaid."

"Come along, then, we must search out the paintings."

"I'm sure I've better things to do, since you'll all be wanting your tea on time."

"Nonsense. This will only take a few minutes. I remember there used to be a severe portrait of some ancestor in a dark robe with a ruffle around his neck hanging over the mantel in the study. I thought it was high time it graced another wall."

"Yes, Sir Hugh said it was a Van Dyck. Very old-like."

"Quite so. The room needed brightening up. I took Sir Hugh to see some Impressionist art works back when I first met him. He rather liked them and we had such a marvelous time choosing. I think he enjoyed the price haggling more than the paintings, but there you are."

"So where are they, then? I've not got all day to be traipsing about."

"I'm not sure. I left before they were hung. One ought to have been placed in the study, and another in the library. Young John Boddy has been tossing Picassos into the mix, so Heaven knows where they are now. Let's browse around, shall we?"

Mrs. Peacock took Mrs. White by the elbow and pulled her away from the kitchen sink. "Hugh favored Manet. I prefer Monet. We agreed on Renoir. Hugh had been hinting about a surprise gift when I left to go to Cambridge. I was amazed at how easily he was able to purchase exactly the paintings he wished. Such a shrewd negotiator. My favorite Renoir was in the Louvre in Paris. He wrote to say he had purchased it for me. I don't know how he persuaded them to part with it."

They proceeded along the passageways to the study. Mrs. Peacock sensed reticence in her guide, but there was no one else she could ask. One could hardly bring John Boddy's attention to paintings if one had designs on them. Mrs. White used her apron to swipe dust off the occasional tables as she passed, as if she hadn't a moment to spare from her duties.

"The first one I'm looking for is Hugh's Manet. A young couple in a sailboat, the water receding endlessly behind them, her hat a fluffy mix of black and white. That was why Sir Hugh liked Manet—the other Impressionists didn't use black, but Manet did."

"Sir Hugh had a black heart." Mrs. White smoothed her apron and glanced at her watch. "That one's in the study. I'll bet you liked her hat, too. A bit feathery, like yours."

"Hugh was a wonderful kind man, not a black bone in his body." Mrs. Peacock hastened her steps to the study. There it was, the Manet, clean and crisp as she remembered it. "I cherish my memories of Hugh, and our days together at the galleries. Isn't this a marvelous piece of art? I am so happy to find it safe and sound, if underappreciated."

"I'm sure Master Boddy appreciates it. He was asking about it just the other day. Will that be all?"

"No, I need to find the other two. Shall we search the library?"

The sunlight filtering in through the library's lace drapes fell in a dim pool over the reading tables.

"You see, this room screams for cheeriness. Those drab pastoral scenes by Gainsborough are so tedious." Mrs. Peacock pointed at them. She was sure Mrs. White didn't know Gainsborough from Scarborough. "And these two by Constable, with his odd patches of bright red, and his blobs of white to show the sun reflecting on the damp wood. Why he didn't just move out into the sunlight and paint something brighter, I don't know. We'll have to see about moving these around. It's too dull in here."

"By 'we' you mean 'me', I'll warrant. I'll put that task on my list of things to do when I'm finished answering the beck and call of you lot. What's next?"

"The Monet. Sailboats on a lake with some buildings on the shore. The reflections in the water rippling, represented by slabs of color, instead of finely painted details. That's what I like about Monet, the quick strokes, the spontaneity of technique. Rather like my own life, decisions made hurriedly."

"That's there." Mrs. White pointed to the painting in question, in a recessed spot between bookcases.

Mrs. Peacock hurried over. It was like finding a long lost friend. She ran her fingers along the frame. "It's such a treat to see it again. And since Hugh bought this for me, I think I should take it with me when I go, don't you agree?"

"You'll answer to Master Boddy if you go pinching the property." Mrs. White glowered in a way that was most unflattering to a woman her age.

Mrs. Peacock pinched her lips on a sharp reprimand. It wouldn't do to irritate Mrs. White unless one wanted to go making one's own meals. Later, a little time with a fruit knife, a quiet transfer to one's luggage, and the Monet would be home with Mummy.

But where was the Renoir?

She remembered it clearly from their day at the Louvre. A girl in a pink gown standing on a swing, chatting to two men in suits and straw hats. Blue shadows danced across her gown, complementing the blue bows down the bodice and skirt. The colors were wrong, but right. Bright blue shadows, yellow and pink for pools of dappled sunlight. The contrast of warm and cool colors suggested the brilliance of a sunny day, while the subjects hovered in the shadows of the trees.

"Let's carry on then, shall we, to find the Renoir?"

"All right, but this is the last one, and then I'm off to the kitchen to make scones. What does it look like?"

"A girl standing on a swing with big blue bows on her dress."

"Right. That one's in the billiard room. Dusted it just the other day."

They proceeded to the billiard room, with its ornate oak billiard table and matching cue rack.

"There, it should be right there." Mrs. White pointed to a large blank spot on the wall.

"Where could it be?" Mrs. Peacock touched the wall with her fingertips. Her Renoir had hung here.

"There it's." Mrs. White pointed to a large framed painting on the floor in the corner, as if someone were taking it down or putting it up.

Beside it, hidden under the billiard table, the body of John Boddy.

Mrs. Peacock clutched her neckline and felt her mouth go dry. "Oh dear. I think he's dead," she said. Mr. Boddy had nearly fallen through the canvas. His arms were flung out as if he had been carrying the painting, and a wrench lay on the floor beside him. Possibly the correct tool for removing a painting from the wall, but how would she know about such things?

"Dead." Mrs. White nodded. "Happen you're right. Poor lad."

"I hope the Renoir isn't damaged."

Mrs. White's eyes flashed from the body to the painting to the empty space on the wall. "Well, I never," she chided. "Taking a painting down without another to put up in its place. Who'd be left to deal with the faded patch on the wall, then? Am I to run in here with emulsion paint and all these mouths to feed? I don't think so. This painting's going right back up here where it belongs, and no two ways about it."

She stepped over the body, hoisted the painting, swung it around and slotted it back into place.

Mrs. Peacock noticed something tucked into the frame on the back of the canvas but dared not ask Mrs. White to pause while she perused it. Better to let the cook return to the kitchen, and inspect the painting later.

Mrs. White brushed her hands on her apron. "That's that, then. You've found your three paintings. Satisfied?"

"Yes, thank you, Mrs. White. You've been most helpful. And I'll find the colonel to look after John."

As Mrs. White trundled away, Mrs. Peacock regarded the body. Dead was dead, no point in dwelling on it. She'd conscript Colonel Mustard to make the appropriate calls. He would be good at that sort of thing. She'd done it for her three husbands, and there was no joy in answering all the police officer's questions. May as well see what was on the back of the painting. Mr. Boddy wasn't going anywhere. A few more minutes twixt finding him and sounding the alarm would make no difference.

The back of the canvas was surprisingly white for something painted in 1876. A faded yellow piece of paper was tucked into the frame. She pulled it out. Someone had written a list in black ink, in French. Well, of course, Renoir would write in French, wouldn't he? It appeared to be a list of colors.

Blanc D'Argent

Jaune de Chrôme

Jaune de Naples

Ocre Jaune

Terre de Sienne Naturelle

Vermillion

Laque de Garance

Vert Veronèse

Vert Emeraude

Bleu de Cobalt

Bleu D'Outremer

She translated the list, haltingly, to be sure, but at least she knew enough French to get by in polite society, not like her daughter whose foreign language skills were nonexistent because she couldn't manage to behave long enough to graduate from Miss Puce's School for Girls.

Silver White

Chrome Yellow

Naples Yellow

Yellow Ochre

Raw Sienna

Vermilion Red

Madder Lake

Veronese Green

Viridian Green

Cobalt Blue

French Blue

Such glorious colors. She tucked the paper back in the frame, re-hung the painting and considered the brush strokes, the colors laid side by side instead of blended. Somehow, it didn't quite look like she remembered it in the gallery, but that was twenty-five years ago. The lighting was different here. No, it was something else. The man's suit was a little too black, and the shadows on the girl's dress too grey. Perhaps that happened over time. Teams of art restorers kept themselves in business brightening up old paintings.

"I say, admiring the Renoir, are we?" Professor Plum materialized at her elbow. "Fine collection Boddy's got here. It'll be worth a tidy sum."

"I'm afraid it won't do him much good." She pointed at the body. Plum hadn't seen it for the billiard table.

Professor Plum looked distressed. "My, my. Bad roll of life's dice, what? And so close to his birthday, when he would inherit all this and more."

"I feel we ought to call on Colonel Mustard to look after things."

"Excellent idea. Move to the top of the class, Mrs. Peacock."

"Class? You're not teaching at Oxford any more, Professor."

"What's all this in aid of?" Colonel Mustard boomed at them from the door. "Touring the art, are we?"

"Examining the Renoir."

Colonel Mustard sniffed. "Not much use for those Impressionists. I wouldn't give you tuppence for that canvas, even with the provenance. Give me a good old Goya any day, the man was a genius with battle scenes."

"I'm afraid we'll have to keep our tuppences for the moment." Professor Plum pointed at the floor. "Boddy seems to have snuffed it."

The colonel stepped forward with a sharp click of his heels, peered around the table and jabbed his riding crop at Mr. Boddy's leg. "Heave to, then. Clear the area. There's a man's work to be done here. Professor, if you would escort the lady elsewhere."

Mrs. Peacock linked her arm over Plum's and together they strolled to the library. Mr. Green and Miss Scarlet sat at one of the smaller reading tables playing cribbage. Miss Scarlet's marker was way ahead on the board. When she looked up at the newcomers, Mr. Green quickly moved his marker ahead a few pegs. Mrs. Peacock smiled. If the Reverend planned to win, he'd have to deal with the tantrum when Josephine lost.

"This is my Monet," Mrs. Peacock said, steering Plum away from the cribbage table. One needed to be outside of flinging range when the tantrum started. "Sir Hugh and I went on a little shopping spree in 1901. It took him months to close the deal. I suspect the Louvre doesn't like to part with paintings, but Sir Hugh was most persuasive."

"The blue of the sky and water almost matches your dress. Why, if you stand very close to it, I'll think you're part of the painting."

"You are too kind. I believe it's called French blue. It has a translucent quality that makes it excellent for depicting water."

"Renoir includes French blue on his shopping list for paints." Plum said. "I suspect it was one of his favorite colors, too."

"Indeed it was."

"How do you know that, Professor?" Miss Scarlet asked. "About the shopping list. Do the artists write the lists on the backs of the canvases?"

"No, but Renoir's list is tucked into the frame of the painting. Quite a rarity. The list increases the value of the painting."

"Shall we take a look, then?" Miss Scarlet asked.

"It wouldn't do you any good to look. The list is in French," Mrs. Peacock said. "You don't know any French."

"Of course I know French," Miss Scarlet replied. "*Mademoiselle est elegante dans la petite robe noire.*"

"Ah-ha. *You look divine in that little black dress.* Excellent, Miss Scarlet. Move to the top of the class." Professor Plum clapped his hands.

"Class? I'm not at Miss Puce's anymore."

Colonel Mustard strutted in. "All taken care of, my good people, in jig time. We'll not be delayed for lunch." He snapped open a newspaper and sat in a straight-backed chair. "Hmm, it says here some American named Charles Lindbergh has been mucking about with aeroplanes, says he can fly across the Atlantic. Shouldn't want to try it myself. I'm reminded of the time Billy Bishop and the Red Baron were dueling it out."

Mrs. Peacock excused herself and slipped away to the study. She could not abide those tedious war stories. She'd rather admire her paintings. She stopped in front of Sir Hugh's Manet. Such a fine painting, with the girl coyly leaning back in the boat, and the young man hardly able to keep his eyes off her. Another pretty blue dress, although the hat didn't go with it, shades of white with a black ribbon. What was she thinking?

Did the hat belong to her little black dress, her *petite robe noire*?

Of course. That was what bothered her about the Renoir.

What was it Colonel Mustard had said about the Renoir? He wouldn't give tuppence for it even with the provenance.

The useful thing about wearing a hat was one always had access to a hatpin. She sat down at Boddy's desk and poked at the locks on the drawers until they sprang open. Boddy had a lot of files. One would think he had been collecting dossiers on people. Methodical, meticulous notes, alphabetically arranged. She would look under P for Peacock later. For now, she restricted herself to A for Art. She didn't want to be late for tea because she had squandered her time. It didn't do to get a reputation for being less than punctual, a fact that seemed lost on Josephine.

Here it was. The provenance on the Renoir, detailed on the letterhead of Oxford University, dated 1914. A delightful description followed. *Girl on a swing, vermilion and silver white mix dress, cobalt blue bows, French blue shadows on dress.*

One of her favorite colors, French blue. A translucent blue that shimmered in the sun when rendered in silk. Those were the colors listed on the paper in the back of the painting, all the colors the artist had chosen.

Right.

She shoved the papers back into the drawer and marched back into the library. She stopped in the middle of the room and pointed her hatpin.

"I accuse you of murdering Mr. Boddy in the billiard room with the wrench."

A WHITER SHADE OF BLUE

SOLUTION:

"Only four people saw the painting off the wall—Boddy, Mrs. White, myself, and the killer. Boddy is dead so he didn't tell anyone. Mrs. White stayed in front of the painting. I know because I was in the room with her. Only the killer and I saw the slip of paper tucked in the frame. You, Professor Plum, had read the list of paints."

"But why would I kill Mr. Boddy because of an artist's palette?" Professor Plum's eyebrows arched.

"Because that Renoir is a forgery. Renoir used bright blue instead of black to paint shadows. Renoir didn't use black at all; it isn't on the list. Yet the men's suits are black and the shadows are gray. The original painting is at the Louvre. Sir Hugh probably couldn't talk them into selling, so he bought a forgery. When you met him in 1914, you provided him with a fake provenance. You are the only one here who went to Oxford. Mr. Boddy had tracked down the information and was about to expose you."

Mrs. Peacock replaced her hatpin in her hat. She sincerely hoped her Monet was not a forgery. It wouldn't do to take it home if it wasn't real.

PUCE VERSUS NETHER WALLOP

"What is that dreadful smell?" Mrs. Peacock asked, wrinkling her nose at the door to the dining room.

"I was hoping you'd be able to identify it," Mr. Green said, hiding a fish knife in his pocket. "It's coming from the kitchen." He backed against the Welsh dresser, gently pushing the silverware drawer closed.

"Oh dear, that is unfortunate. It smells a little like, let me think, pungent, spicy, earthy, rotten. I am quite at a loss to identify it."

"We'll have to ask Mrs. White. It's probably our dinner."

Mrs. Peacock paled under her perfect makeup and jaunty little blue hat. "I feel I must take a walk in the garden. If you would excuse me." She walked away, a pale blue cotton hanky held at her nose.

Green watched her go. When he heard the front door close, he resumed his exploration of the dining room Welsh dresser. The fish knife was worth a few bob, but he'd need six to make a set, or he'd be laughed out of the pawnbroker's. Just a little spare change, that's all he needed. He considered the design on the handle carefully. It looked like a bunch of swirls, but if it was Sir Hugh Black's initials, or the family insignia, he'd have to keep them in his luggage until he got back to London. The locals would recognize the chattels from the family seat.

"Nicking the knives, are we?"

The voice behind him startled him. Mrs. White had slithered in on soft feet, her hands full of silverware.

"Most certainly not. I am a man of the cloth. Thou shalt not steal. I was merely studying the design. I've an interest in heraldry, and I wondered if this was the Black family crest."

"Nah, it's the fishmongers. He gives the knives as free gifts when you buy a fresh plaice. Everybody has them around here." She walked around the table setting the places for dinner.

"How interesting." Green smoothed his pocket. He'd have to slip them back in to the dresser when Mrs. White turned her back. Right now he needed a distraction. "Fascinating candlestick on the sideboard. It has an intricate design. Is this from the fishmonger, too?"

"No, that's the real thing. Solid silver. Dramatic, isn't it, with the three candles? It's Oliver Cromwell's crest on the base section. One of Sir Hugh's ancestors fought with Cromwell and was given the candlesticks as a gift. Either that or he nicked them on the way home from Cromwell's main camp. Anyroad, we've only the one of the pair. Young Master Boddy took them to boarding school with him and when he came home in disgrace, he'd lost one. "

"I see." He picked up the Cromwellian heirloom and turned it over to read the silversmith's mark. "Why was he sent home in disgrace?"

"They say he'd made off with the headmaster's snuffbox, one presented to him by Queen Victoria on his fifty years of service to Obsidian College." She took the candlestick from his hands and placed it on the table as a centerpiece.

"I've known Boddy several years. He doesn't strike me as one to flout the Lord's rules." Except when he wanted to augment his modest trust fund allowance which was all he had until he inherited the estate on his thirtieth birthday. Perhaps he got his early training at school.

"I wouldn't know about him and rules. I was just the nanny. Wasn't my job to teach him right from wrong. Anyroad, he was expelled and came home in the middle of the school year. Sir Hugh had to pull a few strings to get him into Oxford." She smoothed her apron. "I must get back to the kitchen and see to dinner."

"Tantalizing aroma. What are we having tonight?"

"Boiled lamb chops with garden herbs and onions, and curried parsnips. I thought it might make a nice change from roast beef and mashed potatoes. Besides, the lamb has been hanging about in the icebox for a few weeks. It wants using up."

Green shuddered. Old meat handled badly, and the smell disguised by an accompanying pungent spice. His stomach reeled. If there was one dish Mrs. White did well, it was roast beef and mashed potatoes. It was all that was keeping him alive between bouts of her experimental dishes. The aroma wafting from the kitchen was enough to make a grown man gag, even one who had been served couscous with goat's eyeballs in Morocco.

Some charm was in order. "Mrs. White, you make the most divine roast beef. I do hope we see its return tomorrow night. With your mouth-watering Yorkshire pudding." He felt his mouth watering as he spoke, but more from imminent nausea than thoughts of future culinary delights.

"Flatterer." Mrs. White waved him away with a smile bordering on winsome. "I dare say you'd charm the apples off a tree. But I'll promise you roast beef tomorrow, then. It's a sight easier than this foreign cooking, I can tell you. Toss it in the Aga cooker and come back when it's done. You know, I think I should pick some mint from the garden to sprinkle on the chops."

She left for the kitchen. He emptied his pockets of fish knives and turned his attention to the candlestick. Cromwell, handed down through several generations of the Black family. A good provenance. But only half of the pair, enough for a week in London at the Farflung Arms, or a month in Tunisia. He'd have to search for something else if he wanted a week at the Savoy. Onward to the study.

On the way he met Mrs. Peacock in the hall.

"It's boiled lamb chops and curried parsnips," he told her.

She jammed her hanky to her mouth and fled.

Green arrived at the study and peeped through the crack in the door. The coast was clear. Boddy was not in his study. He slipped in and rifled through the desk. Lots of papers, nothing pawnable. No silver card case or brass pen holder. There might be a wall safe in this room behind a painting, but he'd need a definite plan to crack it. That was a task for another day. Maybe this gold letter opener was worth something.

From the back of the house he heard a scream. He put the letter opener down and joined the other running feet heading for the dining room.

He was the last to arrive. Mrs. White stood in a circle of mint leaves, scattered like rose petals at a wedding, with a lumpy glob of something yellow on her right shoe and slimy gray slabs of meat on her left.

On the floor near the Welsh dresser lay Boddy. By all appearances, someone had coshed him with a large ornate silver candlestick with three candles and Cromwell's crest. It lay beside his left hand.

Colonel Mustard poked the body with his riding crop. "Did not survive, I declare. Authorities must be called. Stand clear."

"What is that awful yellow mess on the floor?" Miss Scarlet asked. "It smells dreadful."

"That's your dinner, that's what it is. I was just bringing it to the table. All afternoon I've been cooking, and now it's ruined."

"Never mind, Mrs. White," Mrs. Peacock said. "I'm sure we're too upset to eat. Some toast and jam in the lounge would do."

"We could all go down to the local for fish and chips," Professor Plum said. "I hear they put on a rather good spread."

"I feel the Lord's presence." Green raised his arms and his voice heavenward. Professing to be a clergyman came in handy with opportunities like this. "I feel the power of grace calling the soul of the departed." He knelt beside the body. "Let us pray."

They all bowed their heads. Worked every time. People were afraid to challenge an impromptu prayer meeting. He chanted a string of Latin and Spanish he'd learned at the Seminary and in the bars near it while he tucked the candlestick under the back of his jacket. As they all had their eyes closed, they didn't see him. All he had to do was remain facing everyone. When he had a secure grip on the base by his hands clasped behind his back, he droned, "Amen."

"Stand clear, now. Out, all of you out. I must have a secure area here." Colonel Mustard used his riding crop to whisk them away. Miss Scarlet and Mrs. Peacock hurried into the passageway, with relieved looks on their faces and Professor Plum on their heels.

Green nodded to Mrs. White. "You've had a shock. Let me help you to the kitchen. You can make tea. It will take your mind off this tragedy." He bowed slightly and used one hand to indicate she should precede him.

Once he had her safely in front of him in the kitchen he slipped the candlestick into the closest cupboard. "Now, Mrs. White, tea will settle your nerves after losing Boddy and the parsnips in one go. How about having a lemon tart? I'll get the tarts from the cupboard, shall I, while you put on the kettle."

Mrs. White nodded and filled the kettle at the sink. Green opened several cupboard doors and left them ajar under the ruse of seeking the tarts. He retrieved the candlestick, slipped out the door, ducked into the ballroom, and stashed the candlestick in a potted palm. The Lord helps them that help themselves. He tiptoed back into the kitchen and made some noise rummaging for the tarts.

"—spent a lifetime, didn't they? Did you find it? Under the flour sack." Mrs. White was saying on his return.

He lifted the flour sack, fifty pounds at least, and found nothing but a worn overstuffed scrapbook. He pulled it out, replaced the flour, and brushed the flour dust from his silk suit. Really, the things he had to put up with in the middle of a good heist.

"Is this it?" he asked. "I'll bring the tarts."

"Of course it's. Have you never seen a scrapbook before? There's many a happy memory there." She set two cups of tea on the table, sat down beside him and turned the pages. "That's Master John when he first came to Tudor Hall. Skinny lad, wasn't he? Never was able to fatten him up. That's the newspaper account of his parents' disappearance. That's him off to boarding school. That's him in the Christmas pageant. Winslow drove me down to watch it. Ever so sweet, it was, with Master Boddy playing the innkeeper who didn't like company. Here's Master Boddy at sixteen, stage manager for the Better Schools Drama Competition. I didn't get to see that one, my Winslow had died. Here's the newspaper article about the theft."

"Theft?"

"Yes, I already told you, the Headmaster's prized snuffbox. It was part of the props on the mantelpiece for the performance of 'All's Well That Ends Without Crying', by Miss Puce's School for Girls, and for 'A

Midsummer Night's Yachting' by the Nether Wallop Compulsory School. Nether Wallop won the competition. Here's the newspaper clipping with the photos of the performances and the presentation of the cup to the Wallop cast."

Green pulled the scrapbook closer and read the theft article. "It says here Master John Boddy claimed he didn't steal the snuffbox."

"So he said, but as stage manager, the props were his responsibility, so they expelled him. The Headmaster was right miffed about it, being as Queen Victoria was dead by then and couldn't give him another. Look, in the photo of the play by Nether Wallop, you can see the snuffbox on the mantel between the candlesticks. And mind you don't get tart crumbs on my scrapbook."

Green took a close look at the newspaper photo. He'd swear those candlesticks were the Cromwell set. "Look here, Mrs. White. Aren't those the Cromwell candlesticks?"

She leaned over the photo. "Why, yes. I packed them in his trunk when he left for school, in case he needed a light in his room, poor lad."

"And he returned with only one. In the meantime, he'd used them as props for the play, along with the snuffbox."

"Happen you're right there, Reverend."

"The snuffbox disappeared. The candlestick must have disappeared at the same time. Didn't anyone notice?"

"The headmaster didn't, he was all atwitter about his snuffbox. Master Boddy hadn't asked to use the snuffbox, you see, he just went around acquiring suitable items for the sets. Master Boddy didn't mention the candlestick being missing. Sir Hugh didn't notice. I saw we were missing one when I unpacked the young master's trunk, but I thought no more about it. Never liked polishing that set. All twiddly bits. Care for another tart?"

"Don't mind if I do. Your baking would melt the heart of an angel." Her other cooking would send the devil screaming into the fires of hell, but he didn't feel this was the right time to bring that up. "A shame, really, about the candlestick. They'd have made a handsome pair on the dining table."

"Yes, that they would. Finished your tea? I've to get on with making toast and jam for dinner now, according to that Mrs. Peacock. Don't know if I've the heart for anything else, anyway."

Green excused himself and left the kitchen through the dining room door. He found Colonel Mustard standing guard over the body, candlestick in hand. Foiled again. "How are you getting on, Mustard?"

"Authorities will be here momentarily. I'll stand down then and let them take charge." He lifted his arm to show his trophy. "Noticed right off the candlestick had gone amiss. Had the devil of a time finding it. Searched three rooms and finally found it staring me in the face in the ballroom on the grand piano. Sitting there like it was all set for a performance. Seemed like it had been there for years. I took no notice first time I looked. Second time, I noted there weren't any candles in it. That's military training for you, attention to detail. See here, one of the candle-holding fronds was bent in the attack." He pointed to the offending frond.

Green took a careful look. He was sure the candlestick he'd hidden didn't have a bent frond. That would lessen the value. He'd have noticed a detail like that, with his training in the rapid assessment of fenceable goods. "I'll let you get on with things, then," he said, and left the room.

When he was sure the coast was clear in the passageway, he skulked into the ballroom. There, still jammed in the potted palm pot, was his candlestick. So there were two in the house, after several years of one being missing. He recalled the scene in the dining room when he'd been inspecting the knives. The candlestick originated on the sideboard. Mrs. White had placed it on the dining table. Later, when they found John, the candlestick lay on the floor by his left hand. Was it the same candlestick? At what point had the second come to light? He'd have to do some snooping. He'd search the rooms, ask a few questions. There could be money in this for him, once he tracked their movements. It was often risky stealing something that had already been stolen.

He slipped out of the room and peered down the passageway. Colonel Mustard was stationed outside the dining room door. He could hear the voices of the authorities behind the door. He stuffed his hands in his pockets like he'd been innocently wandering around.

"Unfortunate turn of events, this, don't you think, Colonel?" he said.

"Indeed, sir. A rum business. A disgrace to honest folk." Colonel Mustard stiffened to attention.

"I was talking to Mrs. White, and she mentioned the time Boddy was sent home from school in disgrace," Green said. "Do you remember that incident?"

Colonel Mustard harrumphed. "I was visiting Sir Hugh at the time. Boddy came home with all his kit, not as much kit as those women brought for this holiday, mind. Just a trunk and a satchel he had. Travel light, myself. A carpetbag is all I need. But there's the lad, standing at the front door, cap in hand. Hugh was outraged. Didn't want the boy underfoot for the rest of the term. Got on the telephone and gave the Headmaster what for. I knew what to do. Put the boy in military school, I said, give him some backbone. Teach him right from wrong."

"Then what happened?"

"Upshot was Hugh managed to pull enough strings to get the boy into

Oxford. Got the Obsidian Headmaster to drop his complaint about the snuffbox. Paid him off, I expect. These scholarly types are not averse to taking a little under the table when it comes their way. Poorly paid, you see, and no sense of honor." He tightened his rigid stance. "Honor between gentlemen, that's the ticket."

"Quite so. Thank you, Colonel. I'll keep that in mind." Green wandered down the hall. He would have whistled but that would have been uncouth.

He found Mrs. Peacock in the conservatory sniffing the flowers in turn.

"Excuse me, Mrs. Peacock, I wonder if I might have a word?" he said.

"How about perfunctory, or aromatic, or repertory? Those are all good words. Would you like any of them?" She snapped the head of a dead flower and dropped it in its pot.

"I'll borrow repertory, if I might. Such a full word. Conjures up an entire season of enjoyment. I'm sure you take in the theatre season regularly. I wonder if you ever had cause to attend the Better Schools Drama Competition? I hear it's quite good."

"Actually it's quite dreary." She turned away from the flowers and ran her fingers along a leaf of the split-leaf philodendron. "I went one year because my daughter Josephine was in a play with Miss Puce's School. It was quite dreadfully amateurish. In the lead role Josephine was visually pleasing but appallingly bad as an actress. She had no feel for timing, or presence, or even acting in character. For that matter, she didn't even know her lines. I was humiliated. I marched up on the stage afterwards to tell her so, but she flitted off before I caught her."

"Do you remember the sets for the plays?"

"Of course I do. There was nothing else to amuse myself with while I suffered through it, act by stultifying act. Papier mâché fireplace, seedy furniture from the staff lounge of the host college, silver candlesticks, Tiffany lamps, ratty rugs from the dorm rooms, judging by the stains."

"Were the candlesticks there at the end of the show?"

"They were there when the curtain came down. I was staring at them, wondering if dripping candle wax would be difficult to remove from the leaf fronds at the base of each separate candleholder. One has to amuse oneself somehow."

"Were they there when you left the stage after seeking your daughter?"

Mrs. Peacock glared at him. "What an impudent question. I shall not answer it." She turned her back on him and marched away to study the fish tank with intense concentration.

He couldn't be bothered pouring out the amount of charm the situation required, so he moved on.

He found Professor Plum in the billiard room, pushing the balls around with the wrong end of the cue. "Sad affair, this, isn't it?" he said. "Don't quite know how to act. I ought to have gone to drama school. I always liked the idea of being someone else for three acts."

Plum nodded. "I say, I feel the same way. I thought I'd come in here for a little quiet game, keep out of the way, lie low, as it were. I dare say you're right. Acting school would have come in handy."

"I wonder if you were ever at the Better Schools Drama Competition?"

"Yes, yes, I went a couple of years when I was first teaching at Oxford. They liked to keep an eye out for the cream, you see, and I was to spot students who looked like Oxford material."

"Did you find any?"

"Yes, one year I spotted a couple of lads from Nether Wallop, they were in the winning play. Had a chat with them on stage after the show. I believe they joined us the next year."

"How about any from Miss Puce's school?"

"There was one, a chubby little girl, seemed quite bright. They had this other girl, very pretty but hopeless on the stage. Couldn't remember her lines. The play was so boring I left halfway through."

"Do you remember the sets for the play? Do you remember the fake fireplace?"

"Fake? Do you really think so? It was dashed realistic looking to me, right down to the candlesticks and trinket box. If that was fake, someone had done a fine job building it."

Green smiled. "I'm sure I'm mistaken. I wasn't there, only heard about it. I must have heard wrong. And here I am, going on at length about nothing, interrupting your game of skill. I'll be off."

That had gained him nothing but confirmation of other facts. He found Miss Scarlet in the lounge, pacing the floor.

"Hello, Reverend. Just practicing my walk. In case I get a call from Noel Coward. You have to practice your craft or you get rusty, don't you think?"

Rusty, indeed, trying to snatch worthless fish knives. "Yes, I do understand. Your walk appears polished. I'm sure you are an accomplished performer Mr. Coward would be delighted to employ. I was talking to Mrs. White about a marvelous performance you gave in a play you were in several years ago, in school."

"Oh, yes, I was rather good even then. I had the lead role in 'All's Well That Ends Without Crying'. We entered the play competition with it. We didn't win, though, and I thought that was unfair. We were clearly the best. The next year I didn't get a role at all in the competition play. The Headmistress said she had to give every girl a chance, so even though I was the obvious choice, I had to be skipped over in favor of some other girl. They won that year. And a smug lot they were too, when they came home." She turned and walked away from him, her smooth swaying steps only slightly marred by her turning her ankle when she reached the pattern on the Oriental rug.

Green sat down for a few minutes and pretended to read the newspaper. So far he had learned that the Cromwell candlesticks were on the stage during the performances, and gone some time after the final curtain after the presentation of the award. Most of the guests at Tudor Hall had been at the performance, and on the stage at some point. He wasn't sure exactly when the candlestick had been pinched.

What to do next? Someone had brought the candlestick to the mansion, possibly with the intent of returning it unobtrusively, or finding its match and pawning it as a set. He ought to search the rooms for signs of candlestick smuggling. Perhaps he'd find the imprint of three candleholders with leaf fronds in someone's nightwear, or a big wad of wrapping tissue.

Green smiled at Miss Scarlet, took an obvious glance at his watch, and left the room. He carried on his snooping upstairs.

In the lilac room he found two small shabby cardboard suitcases, held together with tape. Neither was big enough to hold a candlestick. The contents of the cases were hung in the wardrobe or tossed on the dresser.

In the yellow bedroom, he found a carpetbag. Not long enough to hold a candlestick. It was empty, and the former contents color coded neatly in the wardrobe or aligned on the dresser in descending order of size.

In the pink room, and in the blue room, he was met with a veritable wall of luggage, trunks, hatboxes, and suitcases. It looked like certain people planned to stay for several months, or had no other place to call home and were carrying about all their worldly goods. It also appeared as if certain people were expecting Mrs. White to unpack for them, and hang all the lovely things in the wardrobe. The blue luggage was relatively tidy, but the top layers of the pink luggage were scattered about.

Plenty of space in these trunks to hide a candlestick. He set to work. His search skills were not too rusty. He worked quickly and quietly. His hands slipping between folds of silk and satin warned him that other hands had done the same thing recently, as the clothing was no longer crushed together as it would have been after transit. His efficiency was soon rewarded. Jackpot. In a little black bag he found a snuffbox. Inscribed.

He slipped it in his pocket and promenaded down to the front hall, where the other guests were milling around putting on gloves.

"Do join us, Green," Plum said. "We're going to the local for fish and chips."

He threw himself in front of the door with arms outstretched. "Not so fast," he said. "I accuse you of murdering Mr. Boddy in the dining room with the candlestick."

Puce Versus Nether Wallop

Solution:

"I did not," Miss Scarlet said. "Why would you think such a nasty thing?"

"Because one of the Cromwell candlesticks has been missing for several years, and today it was found in your luggage."

"Did John tell you? He said he didn't tell anyone, just came straight to confront me. I was in the dining room, hoping to find some coffee."

"I imagine he was quite angry at you."

"Yes, he was. I didn't know why, it was just a silly old candlestick."

"Really, Josephine, do you not pay any attention to world events?" Mrs. Peacock asked. "The candlestick disappeared along with the snuff-box, and that made the papers."

"So John said. He said he was expelled from school because of it. He said it was my fault. I didn't know the snuffbox belonged to the headmaster. I thought it belonged to the Nether Wallop cast. I was so disappointed they won the play competition, and they were so smug about it, that I decided to take them down a peg by pinching their props. I grabbed the snuffbox and one candlestick. I only had two hands. I was going to come back for the other candlestick, but by the time I'd hidden my booty, there were people on the stage packing up. John was scratching his head at the mantel, holding the other candlestick."

"When you came to visit here this summer, you brought all your possessions, including the candlestick." Green said. "John found it in your trunks."

"He was going to tell everyone. He was going to clear his name and besmirch mine. If the theatres thought I went around pinching the props as a hobby, they'd never hire me. I'd never work in London again. I grabbed the other candlestick off the sideboard and clobbered him. I heard Mrs. White coming in from the garden, so I took it with me and left it on the piano."

"And he dropped the other one, the formerly missing one. That's the one we found with him, and mistook for the weapon of the moment." Green nodded. "Colonel Mustard was alert to the damage on the candlestick which he found on the piano."

"Quite so, old boy," Colonel Mustard said. "You can't slip anything past these eagle eyes. All in the training, you see."

Green kept his face somber. No one had noticed the discrepancy in facts, that there was still a candlestick unaccounted for. If they did, he'd spirit it out from behind the potted palm and tuck it in Miss Scarlet's trunks. Meanwhile, he had the snuffbox in his pocket, and it would be worth quite a bit to one of his private buyers, who would never read past the line "Presented by Her Majesty Queen Victoria".

SPARKLE AND PLENTY

Miss Josephine Scarlet yawned and rolled over in bed. The sun was bouncing through the windows, ricocheting off the Louis Quatorze mirrored dresser to the crystal chandelier, and zapping her eyes. Must be noon.

She might get up. Or might not. Let John wait for her appearance.

She ran her fingers along the satin sheets of the four-poster bed and gazed at the pink brocade draping. She could do much worse than John Boddy. She could do better, with the Prince of Wales being the most eligible bachelor in the country, but he came with all that excess baggage, all that curtseying and formality and opening bridges. No, John was a prudent choice. Unfettered money. She felt good about her performance casting her lines with hooks last night. Today she would reel him in.

She rolled over and propped herself up so she could see herself in the mirror. She ought to practice her pouting. *John, darling, I simply must have some new shoes.* No, too frowny. *John, darling, I simply must go to London to see my friend Georgia in her new play.* Much better. Well, that was enough practicing.

Time to get on with business. Mother was continuing to be stingy with the purse strings, even though she had to have gobs of money stashed away after three husbands. It was getting tedious, asking her for a few thousand pounds now and then and being greeted with that alarmed look.

If you were to make your own way in life, you had to create your own opportunities. Acting hadn't panned out. Directors kept telling her they'd already cast the parts. Marriage seemed a good alternative. Easier, too, without all that pesky memorizing of lines.

Far in the distance she heard the noon gong. She slipped out of bed into cerise satin slippers and a salmon pink silk dressing gown with silver lace trim. Let John Boddy try to resist that over a bowl of vichyssoise.

Down in the dining room, the others were poised over bowls of something strangely purple. No one was eating. The white damask tablecloth was gone and the tableware was set directly on the mahogany, with the six places evenly spaced along the twenty-foot table.

"Miss Scarlet. Care to try a little of Mrs. White's Scotch broth?" Mr. Green asked. "It's hot and tasty. The Lord giveth."

"If it's so tasty, why is your spoon still clean? Has anyone seen John?"

"Pass the bread, please," Colonel Mustard said. "I last saw Mr. Boddy in his study, on the telephone." He leaned toward Professor Plum, who pushed the breadbasket to arm's length and skittered it the remaining distance.

"I saw him in the front hall, accepting a delivery." Mr. Green smiled. "Something small. I believe I'll have some of that lettuce. Mrs. Peacock, can you reach it?"

"Of course. I'll slide it your way. Josephine, if you'd get up at a reasonable hour, you would have seen John and you wouldn't have to bother everyone at lunch."

"I saw him in the conservatory, practicing some kind of speech,"

Professor Plum said with a sigh, his eyes lingering on Miss Scarlet's left hand. "A very short speech."

Mrs. White brought in another steaming bowl of Scotch broth. "How are you all liking my new recipe? Spent all morning on it, I did. Mind you, I had to make a few substitutions. Scotch broth calls for white cabbage, carrots, turnip, and a neck of mutton. I was a little shy of white cabbage, so I used red cabbage. It looked so pretty I added some beets, eggplant, paprika and rhubarb. Master John should be here by now. It's not like him to be late for a meal."

"I'll go look for him, shall I," Miss Scarlet said. "Just coffee for me at the moment, Mrs. White. I might eat later."

"The table won't be set for lunch later. It'll be set for dinner, and you can't use the fish knives to eat Scotch broth. There is no coffee at this meal. Coffee is served at elevenses. I've no time to crush coffee beans when I'm making lunch."

Miss Scarlet thrust her hands on her hips and stamped a slippered foot. "I want coffee, and I want it now."

Mrs. White shrugged. "There's tea." She returned to the kitchen.

That didn't work very well. Maybe tomorrow she'd get up an hour earlier. She unclenched her fists and selected a delicate rose-pink china teacup and saucer. She wanted to look as fragile as possible. Men always felt they had to protect a delicate woman.

So where had John been seen? Study, hall, conservatory. Drat. She didn't know which room John had been seen in last. The front hall was closest. She stalked along the corridors until she reached the front hall, then slowed down and made a proper entrance, drifting in on a swirl of silk.

The front hall was empty.

How annoying. She opened the front door and glanced around the driveway and gardens. Nothing but grass and trees and gravel. And Colonel Mustard with a bowl of something, pouring it behind a rose bush and slinking back to the side door. A breeze fluttered her silk, and a little bit of colored paper, the torn corner of a delivery slip, drifted past her. *Sparkle and Plenty, Master—*. Master what? Master carpenters, master horsemen, master greengrocers? People should not be so inconsiderate when they were leaving scraps of paper around.

She must continue the search for John immediately. She would not look alluring carrying around an empty teacup. She needed the steam from the tea to create a haunting mist around her face.

The study was next. She repeated her gracious entrance, to another empty room.

This was all too much. She'd be forced to return to the dining room for hotter tea soon.

John's roll-top desk was scattered with papers. So, he was a little disorganized with the accounts. She'd be able to slip bills for shoes and gowns into the midst, and he'd pay them without question. This was looking better every minute. So was the list of businesses on the top page of whatever he'd been doing. Sparkle and Plenty; Glitter, Inc.; Garrard. Oh, my—Garrard was the crown jeweler.

That meant Sparkle and Plenty were Master Jewelers. They had delivered a parcel to John this morning. A small parcel.

She sat down in the red leather chair at John's desk for a moment to think this through. John had lists of jewelers on his desk. He made a phone call. He accepted a small parcel from Sparkle and Plenty. Her charm and beauty had swayed him. It was a ring. A diamond. It had to be. There was no other explanation.

Well, who needed a delicate pink teacup now?

She left it on the desk and hurried to the conservatory. She searched behind the fish tank and the fountain, under the chaise lounge, beside the aspidistra. John and his small parcel were not there.

This was just too frustrating. She'd go back to that crowd of buffoons and demand they tell her where she could find John. One of them was hiding something. One of them must know. The mansion wasn't the biggest in the country, and they'd all been up for hours. If they'd only think, use their brains.

The quickest way to the dining room was through the ballroom. She began running. Drat, the silk of her dressing gown ballooned around her like a parachute, obstructing her view. Trying to keep her eyes on the door ahead, she beat back the silk. Without warning she was pitched head over heels, landing in a frothy heap, satin slippers flung off.

What the—? She struggled out of the tangled silk.

She had tripped over something large and navy blue at the bottom of the stairs.

It looked like a person. Maybe that fawning professor.

She rolled him over. Drat. It was John Boddy.

His face was exceedingly pale. She suspected he was dead. If she'd had a mirror she would have held it under his nose. Why would he be dead at the bottom of the stairs?

She turned and looked up. At the top curve of the stairs she could just make out a rope tied at ankle height between the banister rods. He must have fallen down the stairs.

What was he doing upstairs when she was downstairs?

Oh, my, she was late getting up so he had been on his way to her room. To her room? That wouldn't do. Being found rumpled in her bed wasn't the same as being found artfully disheveled propped against heaps of pillows.

She looked down at poor John. All her plans, gone for nothing. He looked quite dashing in his navy suit. They would have made a handsome couple. She'd have to reconsider the Prince of Wales.

John had something clutched in his hand. A royal blue velvet box, the kind used to hold a small piece of jewelry like a ring. She pulled it free and opened it.

It was empty.

She sat back on her heels, her thoughts reeling in disappointment. Why would John carry around an empty ring box? He wouldn't. Someone else had found him and taken the ring. No, someone had pushed him down the stairs to get the ring. The diamond must be huge.

That diamond belonged to her. She was going to track the villain down and take it back.

She returned to the dining room, where they were all stationed around that awful purple stuff. She helped herself to more tea and sat down at her place.

"Did you find Mr. Boddy, my dear?" Professor Plum asked.

"Yes, I did." She watched their faces closely. Directors were always shouting at her to look perplexed, look frightened, look scared, or look astonished. She'd see what those emotions looked like. "He isn't feeling very chipper."

Professor Plum glanced down into his bowl. "Small wonder, if he's eaten this."

Mrs. Peacock whisked a hat feather away from her cheek. "Small wonder after you kept him up half the night."

Mr. Green pushed his plate away. "Really? Does he need a doctor?"

Colonel Mustard cleared his throat. "A doctor would be just the ticket. Feeling a little poorly myself."

Mrs. White sniffed. "He'd be feeling better if he ate a decent meal. You'll all be feeling poorly by three o'clock, and coming to the kitchen to scrounge scones. Just look at the amount of Scotch broth that's left, after all my hard work this morning."

Colonel Mustard held up his bowl. "Licked mine clean, Mrs. White."

Mrs. Peacock raised an eyebrow. "Enjoyed it in the company of roses, I assume?"

Miss Scarlet clenched her fists. Drat. Their faces didn't change, didn't register emotions. Just a few twitches of eyebrows, widening of eyes, dipping of corners of mouths, wrinkling of noses and grimacing. Nothing she could use to identify the diamond thief.

"Actually, Mr. Boddy's dead."

They all gasped, jaws dropping open, hands slapped against cheeks or throats. Again, nothing to show their feelings. She couldn't tell who already knew.

Colonel Mustard stood up. "I see. I shall go and see to the matter, then, shall I? Where would I find him?"

"In the ballroom," Mrs. Peacock and Mr. Green said together.

Miss Scarlet frowned. No clues at all from this cast. She'd have to do a physical search for the missing ring. Where to start? With whichever of the men would be likely to steal a ring so he could propose to her. That would be Professor Plum. He was always giving her droopy looks.

She made herself a lettuce sandwich and poured more tea while the others finished up and left the room. She took her teacup and moved stealthily down the hall, stalking Professor Plum. She spotted him in the library alone with a newspaper. She stopped in front of him and pointed with outstretched teacup. "I accuse you of killing John Boddy in the ballroom with the rope, and stealing the ring so you could marry me."

Professor Plum dropped his newspaper. That was a guilty sign if ever she saw one.

"My dear young lady. I have no intention of getting married at this time. Why, I'm sure to be off on an archeological dig in the near future, and Egypt is no place for a lady. Unless, of course, you want to marry me and run off to Egypt? Although at the moment I can't afford you. But I do like you, very much."

"Never mind." Miss Scarlet rolled her eyes and dropped her shoulders in an exaggerated fashion, just like they had taught her in ingénue class. It was one of her best moves. The exasperated semi-collapse, she called it. The ESC.

She moved on to the billiard room where she found Mr. Green poking balls around the billiard table like he knew what he was doing. She stopped in front of him and pointed with outstretched teacup. "I accuse you of killing John Boddy in the ballroom with the rope, and stealing the ring so you could marry me."

Mr. Green's arm shot out and his cue smacked the billiard balls all over the place. Several jumped the table and bounced onto the floor. He straightened up and a few beads of sweat glistened on his forehead.

Drat. He didn't look guilty at all. She put down her teacup and folded her arms. Maybe she could stare a confession out of him.

"My dear Miss Scarlet, how could you think such a thing of me? I am a man of the cloth. I would be the one to perform the ceremony, if you were getting married here."

He pulled a large white handkerchief from his pocket to dab his forehead. A ring tumbled from the folds.

Miss Scarlet pounced on it.

"So, I was right. You killed John so you could marry me."

"No, no, I swear he was already dead when I got there. I was passing through the ballroom on my way to the dining room when I saw him. I was going to tell the others, but the ring box was on the floor beside him and I do know a thing or two about shilling, I mean, the investment value of a diamond. I was going to have this appraised for him. For his estate. Truly."

"So what do you think it's worth?" She rolled it over in her hand and slipped it onto her finger. It was a little snug.

"Eighteen-carat yellow gold, half-carat diamond. Simple setting, with an interesting little gold squiggle on one side of the stone. Not worth too much, cash-wise, on the resale market. It's not the Cullinan. Not going to fetch much as a piece of jewelry. Rather boring."

She flapped her ESC at him and left.

Out in the passageway, she held her hand up to the light. At least it was a real diamond. The light sparked off it like fire.

A hand snatched her wrist and another hand seized the ring and yanked it off her finger. "So. I was wondering where that got to." Mrs. White tucked the ring in her apron pocket.

"That's mine! Give it back!"

"It's not yours. It belonged to Margaret Black Boddy, Sir Hugh's sister and Master John's mother. She were wearing it when she disappeared. Don't know how Master John got his hands on it, but it needed the setting repaired. He'd sent it out. Just came back this morning."

"I don't believe you."

"Look, then." Mrs. White pointed to a portrait on the wall. "That's her. And that's the ring."

Miss Scarlet scrutinized the portrait. The young woman looked much like herself, the same cheekbones, the same eyes, the same grace and exquisite beauty. She was wearing a diamond ring, yellow gold band, small diamond, gold squiggle to one side of the setting. Drat.

Well. Now she had nothing. No John and no ring. She'd done the best she could for the ring. She'd make one last try on John's behalf.

Miss Scarlet stepped into the conservatory. She was running out of enthusiasm for this bit of acting, but the show must go on. She made her announcement to the sole occupant, who was reclining on the chaise lounge.

"I accuse you of killing John Boddy in the ballroom with the rope."

Sparkle and Plenty

Solution:

"Really, Josephine, the notions you get." Mrs. Peacock straightened her hat. "Why would I do that?"

"To stop me from marrying him. Although I don't know why. He had a good chunk of money, and this fine mansion. I know I could do better, but I'm so tired of asking you for money all the time and you acting like you can't spare any."

"I can't spare any. Things are a bit tight."

"Oh, pish tosh, Mother. You're just hoarding it." Miss Scarlet flounced onto the nearest chair and deployed her silk gracefully around her ankles.

"I am not."

"You won't give me enough, though, that's for sure. So I decided to marry John and get his money."

"But you can't do that."

"Why not?"

"Because there's a good chance he's your cousin."

"My cousin? I thought John had no siblings and his mother and Sir

Hugh were the only children in that family and—just a minute. If I'm John's cousin, and he's Sir Hugh's nephew, then—"

"Quite right. I believe you are Sir Hugh's daughter."

"You mean, you, and Sir Hugh? Oh, Mother, how could you?"

"Sir Hugh was a most charming man, not to mention single and rich. I'd had a spot of bother with married men before I met him. Wives can be so one-sided in these matters."

"But, what about Daddy?"

"I married James Scarlet immediately after my sojourn with Sir Hugh. James considered himself your father. I never hinted otherwise."

"But why kill John for being my cousin?"

"Think, Josephine. If John the nephew inherits the lot, Josephine the daughter has a greater claim. Rather than fight John in court for the mansion and the money, it seemed easier to push him down the stairs, and then step forward with my claim. There aren't any other relatives, you see. It will be quicker to reach a settlement."

"Leaving me free to continue my pursuit of the Prince of Wales. I'll be considerably more attractive to him if I have my own estate."

"Now you're using your noggin. Clearly you exercised your brain cells at Miss Puce's for something other than chicanery."

"There's only one small problem." Miss Scarlet ran a finger along the lid of the fish tank, pouting her hurt-and-lonely-child facial expression. "I still don't have any money, and it will be months before this case and the probate is settled. Can you spare two hundred pounds?"

Mrs. Peacock's Pen

Mrs. Blanche White began her early afternoon tidy-up in the lounge. People were so inconsiderate. There was a place for everything and everything ought to be in its place. The mantel candlesticks should align with the edges of the painting above it. The broken gray limestone bust of Akhenaten should be equidistant from the white alabaster face cream jar of Tutankhamun and the ebony black leopard of Ramses II. These items were in such disarray it looked like someone had picked each up and replaced it randomly. Honestly, the five guests spent a good portion of their waking hours in the lounge, dropping biscuit crumbs on the Oriental rug. Had they not noticed the order of things? She began restoring the treasures of the house to their preordained places.

Professor Plum bobbed his head in the door. "I say, Mrs. White, are the afternoon papers here yet? I dropped a quid on Paula-Paulette in the third, and I wondered how she did."

"They should be in the library, as always." Mrs. White frowned at his disappearing backside. How many times did she have to explain to him where and when to find the dailies? That man wandered around with his head in the clouds. She'd a mind to yank on his purple bow tie to bring him back to earth.

Someone had left a silver pen studded with sapphire teardrops on the table beside the green leather easy chair. She sat down for a moment to rest her bunions and examine the pen. It looked expensive. Those were real gems, if she wasn't mistaken, and no doubt about the silver. She'd polished enough of it in her day to recognize it when she saw it. There was a little smooth patch on one side with engraving. *For My Lovely Wife.*

Winslow, rest his soul, had never bought her a gift like that. She tucked it in her apron pocket. A little silver polish and it would be sparkling.

"Excuse me, Mrs. White, have you seen the afternoon papers?" Mr. Green twitched his chartreuse silk jacket straight.

"Try the library. Professor Plum is checking to see if his horse came in. Do you have a wager on Paula-Paulette, too?"

"I know a good horse, and she's not one. I'd be surprised if she did better than Lime Rickey. I, however, placed no bets. Betting the horses is gambling, and gambling is the work of the Devil. I'll be praying for Plum's soul."

"Good luck to you, then."

When he left, she glanced around the room. What else was out of place? Yesterday's papers, strewn on the table beside her. Open to the racing pages. Someone's notes scribbled in the margins in a spindly hand. *Lime Rickey. Good horse, good rider. Twenty-to-one odds on. Place bet on account with village bookmaker.*

Dear Winslow, rest his soul, liked to bet the horses. Let's see, which would he have backed? Paula-Paulette had a good jockey but questionable bloodlines. Lime Rickey had good breeding but the jockey had been known to throw a race. Dash Dot Dash looked like a solid contender, good breeding and reliable jockey. Winslow would have put a bob on Dash Dot Dash.

Too bad the race was over or she might have played it. No, too close to payday. She was nearly skint.

"Mrs. White? Have you seen my pen?" Mrs. Peacock sashayed into the lounge with a writing tablet under her arm. A powder blue scarf clipped to her temples trailed across her shoulders. "Silver, with small sapphires. Sir Matthew gave it to me on our first anniversary."

"Can't say as I have, ma'am. Where did you have it last?"

"I loaned it to Plum. He was working the crossword. He was sitting right there."

She pointed an accusing finger at the leather easy chair.

Mrs. White felt down between the cushion and the arm. "Nothing here. No wait, what's this?" She pulled a newspaper free and unfolded it. A neat square script filled in the blanks of the puzzle. Some were obviously wrong, unless 'rpedenk' was a word. "Only the crossword. No pen, I'm afraid."

Mrs. Peacock seemed perplexed. She began peeping behind the candlesticks, leaving them out of place.

Mrs. White got up and left the room. She'd have to redo the lounge later, when that woman finished fiddling with the knick-knacks. She'd another hour to finish the tidy-up, at this rate, and dinner to cook and all.

Things seemed in order in the hall, unless you counted the fingerprints all over the armor's helmet. It looked like someone had twisted it off. Perhaps someone fancied himself as a knight, and tried it on for size. She used her dust cloth to buff it clean. No sense of order, these people.

The study was in complete disarray. Some papers had fallen off the desk. The telephone was off the hook. A painting sagged away from the wall. Master Boddy lay stretched on the maroon rug, a huge bump on the back of his head, and a wrench near his feet.

She stopped and stared at him. He wasn't breathing. He was dead white, possibly because he was dead. One less person for her to tidy up after. What to do? She'd have to find Colonel Mustard. As an old army man, he'd know how to supervise this affair. She had only poor Winslow's demise as an example of protocol, and Sir Hugh had handled all that. So that was the answer. Ask a man to look after it.

First, though, she'd better tidy up this room. She hung up the phone. She picked up all the papers and placed them in a square pile on the desk. She straightened the painting.

It refused to be straightened.

She peered behind it. A secret wall safe. The door had been jimmied open by something large and metal, judging by the scrapings. She peeked inside. There were many papers, and a black tin box. An empty black tin box.

That was the box Sir Hugh and then Master Boddy carried to the kitchen on payday. It contained her wages, plus the money to cover all the accounts due.

Someone had taken her money.

She closed the safe and straightened the painting. She would get to the bottom of this before the thief had a chance to go to the village for a shopping spree.

She heard voices echoing down the passageway from the conservatory. When she reached the doorway she saw they were dipping into her shortbread tin. No wonder they never ate much dinner!

Professor Plum tried to hide the tin. Miss Scarlet brazened it out, holding the shortbread firmly and taking a big bite with obvious licking of fingers.

Mrs. White ignored the challenge. "I seem to be running low on sugar. I wonder if anyone was planning a walk into the village today, and might pick some up."

Mrs. Peacock shook her head. "There is nothing in that village that interests me."

"I am," Professor Plum said. "I've got to go and see if my horse came in. I can't find today's papers. I walked down yesterday to place the bets, and it was most invigorating."

"Who did you wager?" Colonel Mustard asked. "I heard Lime Rickey was in the running, pretty fair odds, but that jockey often has his head turned by a little offer of cash under the table. I'd put my money on any horse jockeyed by Gordon Richards. I'm sure we'll see him win the Derby in the future."

"I like to bet on the horses," Miss Scarlet said, "but I prefer to go to the track. There are lot of eligible bachelors at the track."

Mrs. Peacock nodded. "I enjoy a social afternoon at the track, although I don't like betting. Handling money and those racing stubs leads to filth on one's gloves. One never knows where those papers have been."

"If only I could find the papers. Has anyone seen them?" Professor Plum pulled a racing stub from his pocket. "I'd really like to find out if Paula-Paulette won."

"They're in the library, I'm sure," Mrs. White said. "I'll have a look, shall I?"

"Sugar? Does that mean you're going to make more shortbread?" Miss Scarlet asked. "We seem to be near the bottom of the tin."

Mrs. White nodded. Clearly Miss Scarlet had never been shopping. Everyone knew perfect shortbread like that was imported from Scotland, and Master Boddy didn't mind paying for it either. Oh, yes. Master Boddy. "Colonel Mustard, there's a matter in the study that requires the attention of a gentleman with your credentials. Master Boddy's come a cropper."

"Indeed? Clear the way then. Stand back." He strutted out of the room. She followed him.

In the study, she pointed out the body and stood back while he poked it with his riding crop.

"Quite dead, he is. I'll call the authorities. They'll see to it. Don't you worry, Mrs. White, I'll have it right as rain by teatime. Stand clear, now."

She took another step back and her heel knocked over the wastebasket beside the desk. Another mess, and she'd better clean it up before the constabulary arrived, or it would still be here tomorrow. She swept the papers, mostly RSVP replies, back into the basket, but noticed four torn bits that looked familiar. She laid them on her hand while the Colonel shouted into the telephone. They matched up easily. It was a racing stub, torn in four, as Winslow used to do when his horse lost. Rather a large bet, more than her wages, on a horse named Lime Rickey in the third. She tucked it in her apron pocket.

Leaving the colonel to handle the unpleasantness, she carried on her mission to find the dailies for Professor Plum. If she found them, she could delay his walk to the village while she searched his room for the money. Like as not the papers were in plain view on the table, and he couldn't see for looking.

They weren't. One of last week's papers lay on the table, open to a page with a recipe. Sweet Potato Pie, an exotic dish from the American South, so said the headline. She read it as she wandered out of the room: Sweet potatoes, cinnamon, sugar, cream, pastry. The pastry she could make in a wink. She didn't have any sweet potatoes, but she had plenty of white potatoes, and they would work just fine. Cooked and mashed, the recipe said. Mixed with cinnamon, sugar, and cream. That sounded an odd combination with mashed potatoes, but she'd go along with it.

Maybe a little sage and onion to liven it up.

On her way outside to the garden, she passed the armor in the hall and stopped. When Master Boddy was little, he used to drop marbles in the mouth hole, and Winslow would open the toe to get them back. Someone had played around with the helmet today, she was sure, as those fingerprints weren't there on yesterday's walkabout.

She twisted the helmet off the armor and reached inside. The lost newspaper was wedged in the neck. She pulled it out and flipped to the racing pages. Dash Dot Dash, winner in the third, with Wild Geranium to place and Beach Coral to show. Neither Lime Rickey nor Paula-Paulette had brought home the money. So Professor Plum was out a quid and someone else was out a fair pile of pounds. That someone clearly didn't want the paper, and the evidence of loss, found. Plum was seeking the paper. Therefore the other person, the bettor on Lime Rickey, had hidden it.

She returned to the lounge and retrieved yesterday's paper. The squat handwriting was Plum's as he'd been seen doing the crossword, and he didn't bet on Lime Rickey. The spindly writing belonged to the person who'd made the bet.

Back to the study she went, to the wastebasket. In it were the acceptances of the invitations to spend the summer at Tudor Hall. She flipped through the scented lavender paper, the French-edge pink paper, the plain white paper with regimental letterhead, until she came to the note with the correct handwriting. So. Of all the lying, underhanded…

Mrs. White marched to the kitchen for a knife. She met her quarry in the billiard room and pointed the knife at his throat. "I accuse you of killing Mr. Boddy in the study with a wrench."

Mrs. Peacock's Pen

Solution:

Mr. Green's eyebrows shot up in horror. "Whatever gave you that idea?"

"You bet heavily on Lime Rickey and lost."

"I don't play the horses. That's gambling. Gambling is evil."

"Yes, you did. It's your handwriting on yesterday's paper, making a note to place a bet. Professor Plum went for a walk yesterday and said he had placed the bets. That's more than one, and he only had one racing stub. The other was torn up beside the telephone."

"Who'd tear up a racing stub before they found the results? I'm sure when the paper comes to light we'll find Lime Rickey the winner."

"I found the newspaper in the armor. You lost. You telephoned the bookie, and he wasn't feeling lenient. You needed to pay him, but you didn't have any money. So you went about cracking open the house safe with a wrench. Master Boddy caught you in the act, and you hit him on the head."

Mr. Green sighed. "I was desperate. The bookie was going to expose my debts if I didn't pay my tab. There was hardly any money in the box, anyway. Barely enough to cover what I owe."

"That's my wages you nicked. I'll not stand for it." She waggled the knife at him. "You'll be giving the money back. Right now." She held out her other hand, palm up.

"But I'll be ruined. Please have mercy on a poor humble man of the cloth. Please help me. Lend me the money. I'll pay it back before I leave. I promise before Heaven I'll pay you back." Mr. Green lifted his arms skyward as if he had a direct line of communication with the Higher Power.

He looked so pathetic, she felt herself softening. Mrs. Peacock's pen weighed in her apron pocket. If she gave it to him, and he pawned it, he'd probably have enough to cover his debt.

But what a beautiful pen. Winslow, rest his soul, would have given her a pen like that, if he could, and would have engraved it *For My Lovely Wife.*

On the other hand, Green looked so sad and helpless.

"You'll be giving me that money now, if you know what's good for you. I have a better way for you to raise the cash than stealing from a housekeeper."

He reached into his jacket pocket and handed her a wad of folded bills. "Do tell. And please, put the knife down."

She accepted the money and dropped it with the knife into her apron pocket. "Right, then. You're a preacher. Tonight you go down to the village pub and offer your services to young couples who are a little tipsy and feel like getting married. Work for your money."

The Chartreuse Trust

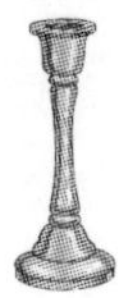

"The Lord's work is sanctified. Give to the Lord. Find charity in your heart and in your purse. The Lord rejoices when even the least of you tithes to the greater glory of goodness. The Lord shall rain blessings upon your house when you give to Him. Blessed are those that give, for it will be given back unto them tenfold."

Professor Plum sank deeper into his gold brocade armchair, hoping to become invisible. Mr. Green was running at full volume, thumping on the lid of the grand piano until the candlestick teetered. His emerald green silk suit crackled with enthusiasm. His pomaded hair jumped and shivered in the morning sunlight streaming through the bay windows. It was a top-drawer show from a man with a suspect claim to being a clergyman.

Plum wondered if he had appeared shimmering and enthusiastic to his students at Oxford. Perhaps not. He'd never summoned this much energy for mummies. Green was itching for a fresh death, which might be more exciting. They were assembled in the ballroom at Green's request for a memorial service for John Boddy, who had been found the previous day stabbed with a knife on the kitchen floor.

That had been one bad day, with policemen all over the kitchen and no food to be had except the tin of imported shortbread cookies Miss Scarlet had hidden behind the fish tank in the conservatory. They'd had to go into the village for their dinner, and the local pub was the only available venue. The food had been wonderful, especially after a few days of Mrs. White's cooking. Plum could still taste the chips and malt vinegar.

The thing of it was the expense. He only had ten quid in cash to last until the now-unnecessary birthday party, when the estate would have been given into Boddy's hands, and, he presumed, a settlement would have been awarded to one Professor Peter Plum for loyal service to Sir Hugh Black. With Boddy's death, the estate would be in tumult for months. Now that ten quid would have to last the summer, or until he found another source of income.

"The word of the Lord is brought to you by men of the cloth. These words are holy words, spoken by the Almighty through the conduit of a mere mortal. Praise the Heavens for these words brought to you at this juncture. Thank the Almighty by opening your hearts to accept His words, and opening your pockets to further the work of God's messengers."

Plum stole glances at the others in the room. Mrs. Peacock was artfully poised at one end of the gold brocade chesterfield, her lilac-gloved hands folded lightly on her lap, the iridescent feathers of her hat rippling in a rainbow of colors. Miss Scarlet sprawled at the other end, looking delightfully disheveled and monumentally bored. Mrs. White sat in one of the upright wooden chairs like an object in a display case. Her fingers twitched at her crisp white apron. Colonel Mustard stood ramrod straight at the back of the room, medals gleaming, eyes alert. Only his riding crop, tapping lightly against his leg, gave him away.

"Praise the Lord, Amen!" Mr. Green boomed.

"Amen," Mrs. Peacock stated and uncrossed her ankles.

Green whipped out a silver plate and began touring the room, holding it before them.

"My handbag is upstairs," Mrs. Peacock said. "If you would excuse me." She rose in perfect grace and swayed out of the ballroom like the Queen.

"Well, I don't have any money, I'm sure," Miss Scarlet said, flouncing away. "You'll have to ask Mother."

"Quite so, quite so, old chap," Colonel Mustard said, patting his pockets. "Don't keep money in my uniform. Not done. Not regulation, you see." He gave Green a tight nod and strode through the door.

"That's not a collection plate, that's a calling card plate," Mrs. White said, snatching the plate from Green's hands. "You don't use it for coins, only cards. Them're too stingy to give, and I've given all my spare cash to the Chartreuse Trust, haven't I?" She straightened the candlestick on the piano and marched away.

Green sat down in a nearby gold brocade chair. "Well, that went well," he said, and his brow creased into a frown.

"I thought it was a very moving service for Boddy. Excellent idea on your part."

"How about you, Plum? Do you have a mite to spare for the poor preacher?"

"Afraid I'm quite drained at present. I've ten pounds to my name. The British Museum let me go, you see, and I'm living from hand to mouth until I find another post. Won't be long, I'm sure."

Green's frown disappeared and he raised an eyebrow. "Have you looked into the Chartreuse Trust? They give grants for academic research and intellectual studies. What's your specialty?"

"Mid-Eastern Culture. I've a strong background in antiquities, especially Egyptian. Did a bit of work for Sir Hugh before he died.

Worked on a retainer from his estate after that. Many of the Egyptian artifacts you see in this mansion are my finds."

"Tell you what, I have a great deal of information on the Chartreuse Trust, it's one of my favorites. I'll find you the forms. If you write up a proposal for research, with an estimate of costs, they give you a grant for that amount to cover it. Once your name comes to the top of the heap, of course. Oh, there's a sign-in fee, it isn't much, nine pounds I believe. Small sum to pay for the chance to receive thousands in grant money."

Plum felt his heart thump. Free money. A modest entry fee, a little paperwork, and then a meal ticket that would last for months. "What sort of return do they look for?"

"A report, an essay, a few photographs, or some artifacts if you're digging. They don't look for results *per se* as much as contributions to the universal well of knowledge."

"I say, that sounds just the ticket. I could use some funding right now."

"There might be a wait, bureaucracy, you know how it goes. They put everyone on a list, and fund them one by one, as the benefactors provide the money. But it shouldn't be too long, I'm sure. I happen to have the forms with me. I'll get you some, shall I?"

"Do, please." Plum settled back in his seat while Green went up the grand staircase to his room. What a pleasant turn of events. All he had to do was come up with a proposed research topic, estimate the amount needed, and the cash would slide into his hands, unencumbered. It was too good to be true. Let's see, now, what would make a suitable topic? Searching for the tomb of Tutankhamen? No, already done. Searching for the tomb of, well, there had to be someone whose tomb hadn't been found yet. He'd just pick a name. It would take an entire season to do a proper dig somewhere. He knew how much that usually cost, because he'd had to keep records for Sir Hugh. He'd double that, give himself room for a few luxuries. If he failed to find anything, he'd apply again for the following season.

"Here you are, then," Green said at his elbow. "Fill out these forms and attach your entry fee, and I'll get it all sent away for you."

"Right you are," Plum said. "Thank you. I am in your debt."

"Think nothing of it. Just bring the cash with the forms." He sauntered away.

Plum gathered the forms and took them to the conservatory where there was a small table he could work on. He dug right in, filling in blanks, adding up figures.

"What are you doing, Plum?"

Miss Scarlet's voice surprised him.

"Filling in forms to get a grant from the Chartreuse Trust."

"I didn't know you were an actor."

"I'm not. I'm a professor of Antiquities."

"That's odd. I applied to the Chartreuse Trust last year. They have a grant for aspiring actors and actresses. For fifty pounds, I was put on the waiting list for guaranteed parts in a season's worth of plays at the theatre of my choice. I got a letter this year saying I was nearing the top of the list, but one of the benefactors had stepped down, and they were replacing him, so I should remain patient. I had to pay an extra twenty pounds for administration fees to retain my spot on the list. What are you applying for?"

"A grant to go on a dig in Egypt. Nine pounds entry fee."

"They certainly are a varied organization." She drifted away.

Plum finished filling in his forms. He was reluctant to provide his full fee. If he used the spending money he had hidden in his sock drawer, he'd have scant left to provide for himself the next time he went to the village. No more fish and chips. He'd be totally dependent on Mrs. White's cooking. Perhaps the Trust would take a smaller deposit, and deduct the rest from the grant. He'd ask Green.

He heard voices in the passageway and followed them to the library. There he found Colonel Mustard and Mrs. Peacock engaged in an argument about the relative merits of secrecy versus full disclosure.

"I say, do you know where Green is?" he asked. "I've filled out these forms for the Chartreuse Trust."

"Excellent organization, that," Mustard said. "Retirement Fund for Officers, Widows, and Orphans. Paid into it for several years. Ought to be seeing a regular stipend from them any day now. They've had a bit of a mix-up in the accounting office, apparently, and will start paying me once the paperwork is straightened out."

Mrs. Peacock raised an elegant eyebrow. "The Chartreuse Trust is a benevolent organization supporting fashion. I've been paying into it for a few years now. I'm a patron of fashion. They tell me the money goes to support new fashion designers, and eventually I'll receive sample dresses. One young designer was perched on the edge of success but his studio burned down, necessitating a delay in my receipt of clothing."

Plum blinked. "This does not sound right at all. Miss Scarlet thinks they are a funding source for aspiring actresses. I was told it was grants for intellectual studies."

Mrs. Peacock looked from him to the Colonel. "We had better ask Green. Let's see if he's in the lounge."

They left the library. Plum sat down at a reading desk. He ought to be able to solve a puzzle like this. He was good at puzzles. While the others were looking for Green, he'd find Mrs. White. She mentioned the Trust at the memorial service.

He found her in the front hall sweeping up the dirt tracked in by the policemen.

"I say, Mrs. White, you mentioned the Chartreuse Trust earlier."

"I did indeed. A fine organization it is, too. I've been pouring me spare money into it for years."

"What does it do, Mrs. White?"

"Its mission is to liberate Scotland from English rule. Give Scotland back to the Scots." She waved her broom like a sword. "Repatriate the Clans. Return the Stone of Scone."

"Oh, my, it sounds like a worthy cause. Have they had any success?"

"Success is just around the corner, they say. There was a bit of a problem with freeing up some important papers from a castle somewhere, which required some extra payments to the solicitors, but they're back on track now."

"As well they should be. Thank you, Mrs. White."

He left her and wandered into the study to think. He sat down at Boddy's desk. There were familiar looking papers poking out of one of the pigeonholes on the roll-top desk. He pulled them out and scanned them. The Chartreuse Trust. He added up the numbers on the several pieces of paper. Rather a large sum of money was involved, debited to the household accounts.

Shouting erupted from the lounge. He hurried to see what the fuss was about. Everyone was there. Mr. Green was backed into a corner, huddled against the green velvet drapes.

"You, sir, are a bounder and a cad." Colonel Mustard waved his riding crop under Mr. Green's nose. "You have misappropriated funds, taken honest money for non-existent causes and foundations. There is no Chartreuse Trust. No Widows and Orphans Fund, no Aspiring Actress grants, no Fashion patronage. We've all been paying into your pocket."

"I want my money back," Miss Scarlet shouted, throwing a cushion at Green. "You mean man. I want my money now, now, now."

"I can explain, really, I can explain." Mr. Green held his hands up to protect himself and his silk suit. "If you just give me a moment, I can explain."

"I accuse you of stabbing Boddy with the knife in the kitchen," Plum shouted.

The Chartreuse Trust

Solution:

All eyes turned to him.

"I didn't kill him," Green said. "He was a benefactor. He paid the Trust fifty pounds a year toward the preservation of stately homes."

"I didn't mean you. I meant Mrs. White."

"Me? Why should I kill my employer?"

"Because you had been paying into the Chartreuse Trust regularly, only you couldn't afford it. So you skimmed money off the household accounts. Boddy discovered the missing money. He was probably going to reclaim it from your wages."

"And me a poor cook and housekeeper these last thirty years. He barely paid me enough to get by on, and now he was going to make me pay it back. I couldn't stand for it, could I? I couldn't let him make me poor and stop me contributing for the cause of Scotland."

Mrs. Peacock shook a finger at Green. "See what problems you've caused. You ought to be ashamed."

Colonel Mustard nodded. "Bogus trust fund. Low blow, sir, low blow."

“Are you telling me the Chartreuse Trust won’t be buying Scotland its freedom?” Mrs. White demanded.

“What’s worse is he didn’t even get me a part in a play,” Miss Scarlet said with a pout.

Plum let them argue with each other. He felt quite vindicated. He’d uncovered the fraud, uncovered the murderer, and saved his own nine pounds.

CLOCKED

Mrs. Peacock sipped her coffee. The lounge was quiet. She and Professor Plum were the first to arrive for elevenses. Plum sank into one of the green leather chairs, his bow tie askew, his tweed elbows worn thin. Really, the man had no social graces at all. She would have to do all the work making conversation with him. Josephine ought to drag herself out of bed and downstairs for the coffee she was always pining for, requesting, demanding. She could chatter on about nothing. Plum would be awed, or at least impressed.

As it was, she'd have to struggle alone to create a congenial atmosphere. She cast about the room for a suitable topic of conversation.

Ah, a china clock on the mantel. She hadn't noticed it before. Mrs. White must be rotating the family finery. It was quite hideous. The tarnished sepia face was surrounded in white china lace and red swirling waves. The whole was festooned in flowers. Bluebells ran up one leg, buttercups up the other. Grapevines entwined around the back legs. Periwinkle, daisies and coral bells circled the face and drooped over the lace at the top. Plump pink carnations and asters cluttered the top, fighting for space with the highest swirl of russet waves.

Nevertheless, it might form a starting point.

After refilling her cup, she strolled to the mantel. "This is an interesting clock, Professor. I hadn't noticed it before. Had you?"

"Hm, what? Oh, the clock. No, no, can't say as I had noticed it. Intriguing design." He shambled out of his chair and joined her at the mantel. "Nice flowers. Pretty." He picked it up with both hands and rolled it over. "Coalport. 1830. The genuine article."

"It must be a recent purchase. It wasn't here yesterday, I'm quite certain."

"Oh, no, nobody would let their old Coalport go now. Factory's closing, you see, after being in continuous operation since 1750. The value just went up."

Mrs. Peacock watched as he turned the clock over in his hands, examining the details. Hideous. With an escalating value. Suppose it doubled, she still wouldn't allow it in her home.

"What would you estimate this one is worth?"

"British clocks are not my line. More of an Egyptian antiquities man. But, this is in excellent condition. Not a scratch. Appears not to have been wound for some time, as the key is still firm. Here's a little scrap of tissue stuck to it, as if the clock had been wrapped up. That explains the condition."

"Coffee, coffee, where's the coffee?" Miss Scarlet swooped into the lounge and bore down on the tea trolley in a hail of crimson taffeta, her dressing gown's wide sleeves almost slicing the shortbread from the plate.

"Good morning, Josephine," Mrs. Peacock said, trying to keep displeasure out of her voice. Really, had they taught her no manners at Miss Puce's School for Girls?

"Nothing good about it until I've had some coffee," Miss Scarlet snapped. "Are there no bigger cups? There's hardly any coffee in the pot. This coffee's cold."

Professor Plum said nothing, just cowered with his back to the mantel and the clock clutched in front of him to ward off evil.

"Josephine, you could at least be civil. There is more than enough coffee."

Miss Scarlet whipped around. "Don't talk to me about civility. Somebody has been pawing through my belongings. I want hot coffee and I want it NOW. NOW!"

She paused, teetering on the edge of her diatribe. "What is THAT doing in here?" She pointed a ferocious crimson sleeve at Plum.

"I came for coffee." Plum swallowed and backed up into the fireplace. "Er, I say, have you seen this clock? Rather a nice clock, isn't it? We just noticed it, on the mantel. Quite valuable, I believe. You might not want to risk it getting broken." He held it tighter to his chest.

"How could you? You low down dirty sneaky rotten—" she snatched a handful of shortbread from the plate and hurled it across the room. The pieces bounced off the mantel, the clock, Plum's tweeds, and Mrs. Peacock's feather hat. "—conniving, putrid, weasely—"

Mrs. Peacock grasped Plum's sleeve and hauled him out of the room. The door swung shut, only serving to muffle the screaming. "We'd best be elsewhere while Josephine has her tantrum. Would you care for a walk in the garden, Professor? I expect there will be flowers in bloom to match that clock."

Mrs. White, proceeding majestically toward them bearing a huge silver tray of fresh coffee and shortbread, gasped. "Well, I never!" She hastily deposited the tray on the closest table. "Well, I never! What are you doing with that clock?"

Plum held it toward her. "Just looking at it, truly, I meant no harm. I'll put it on this table, shall I?"

"You will not. It no more belongs on that table than spit. The lounge mantel is the place for this. After all that time lost, and now this." She nearly wrenched it from his hands. He did not try to hold on.

"Perhaps you might want to find another home for it for the next hour or so, Mrs. White," Mrs. Peacock said. "Josephine has found the coffee not to her liking."

"There's nothing wrong with my coffee. I ground it myself." She pointed to the lead pipe on the silver tray. "Not half an hour ago. This clock belongs on that mantel and that's all there is to it. Right is right."

She brushed past them and marched into the lounge with the clock. As the door swung closed, the screaming grew louder.

"A tour of the garden would be delightful," Plum said, swallowing and glancing back at the closed lounge door. With shaky hands he poured himself another coffee from the abandoned tray.

They proceeded through the front hall, across the gravel driveway to the formal rose gardens. They found a stone bench in the shade of a yew tree and sat.

Mrs. Peacock stifled a sigh. She was back where she started. Trying to make conversation with a post in a purple tweed jacket. "Lovely day, isn't it?"

"Hmm?" he replied.

Mercifully, Colonel Mustard came striding across the garden with a cup of coffee in one hand, his riding crop in the other, marking his progress with sharp digs in the earth. Several rose leaves were impaled on it.

"Bit of a donnybrook in the lounge, time to beat a retreat. Found the coffee in the hall. Spotted you out here. Jolly fine day. Reminds me of the time we were visiting the Raja in the Punjab and had been invited to tea.

The Maharani and I were taking a turn through the gardens when all of a sudden—"

"Have you seen the others, Colonel?" Mrs. Peacock asked. "Mr. Boddy and Mr. Green? People don't usually miss elevenses."

"Met Green at the coffee tray. He heard the row and decided, as a man of the cloth, he ought to intervene and soothe the spirits. Left him to it. Seen more than my share of fighting in my day. As I was saying, the Maharani and I were enjoying a spot of fragrant air when—"

"If you would excuse me, Colonel, I seem to have run out of coffee." Mrs. Peacock got up and walked back to the mansion. Let Plum listen to another crushingly drab story.

Inside the front door she ignored the coffee tray and went straight up the stairs to her suite. If Josephine started breaking things they might be asked to leave. One did not go about willfully destroying the glass and china without penalty. She stopped short at the door. Someone had searched her belongings. Her dresses were scrambled up in her wardrobe and her shoes tumbled out onto the floor. Her hats were out of their boxes.

This was an outrage. She surveyed the damage as she toured the room. Nothing missing she could see, but she'd need to count her jewelry. She set to work. If Josephine's room was in a similar state, well, that explained the tantrum. Explained, but did not excuse. She was livid, too, but she didn't go around throwing shortbread at Plum. Throwing marmalade at Mustard, now that would be rewarding.

An hour later, the lunch gong sounded.

On her way to the dining room, she paused at the lounge to survey the damage. If nothing important was broken, she might be able to get by with some heartfelt apologies.

Shortbread lay sprinkled over the Oriental rug. The Coalport clock was shattered in the hearth. The second coffee tray rested on a small table near the door. John Boddy slouched in the green leather chair, a lead pipe on his lap and a monumental dent in his skull.

She tiptoed into the room. Empty coffee cups and half-full coffee cups sat on all the tables. A family photo lay near Boddy's feet. She picked it up. Sir Hugh and John standing in the lounge in front of the fireplace. John was a youngster, all decked out in his boarding school uniform, his satchel over his shoulder and a suitcase at his feet. Over his head, the family knickknacks were lined up on the mantel. Silver candlesticks, a pottery potpourri vase and the Coalport clock. Why Mrs. White thought they made a nice grouping was anyone's guess. She tucked the photo under her hat.

All in all, limited damage, if one didn't count Boddy. She examined the shards of the clock. The face was intact, and many of the ill-favored flowers. It might be possible to glue it back together again. If she did a clever job, no one would know it had been broken until after she and Josephine had left at the end of the summer. If they were allowed to stay now that Boddy was dead.

Using the hearth broom, she swept all the clock pieces into a piece of newspaper, rolled it up, and hid it inside the drawer of the Louis Quatorze table in the front hall. She hurried along to lunch.

When she arrived at the dining table, they were all seated and staring at something gray in the soup bowls. Mrs. White stood to one side with a ladle and a smug look.

"Here she's now," Mrs. White said. "Haven't I been telling them you'd know what vichyssoise is?"

Mrs. Peacock glanced around as she took her seat. Professor Plum looked exactly as usual. Green looked furtive. Mustard looked agitated.

Josephine looked serene in a salmon crepe dress with matching shawl. She had gotten over her ill temper in enough time to dress properly. "Vichyssoise is a type of cold soup. Usually made with potatoes, onions, chicken stock, and cream."

"Rightly so, but I looked in the ice box and found all that lovely beef gravy from last night, and it was cold, and thick like a cold soup would be. What's the difference between chicken stock and beef gravy, I ask you? It's all a meat source. So I sprinkled some chopped parsley on it for fancy, and there you are—vichyssoise."

Mrs. Peacock thought she could not endure one more exhibition of anger today, so she refrained from commenting on the soup. "John Boddy has had an accident. He's dead. He's in the lounge."

Gasps rippled around the room. Mrs. White dashed for the kitchen. Miss Scarlet pushed her soup bowl away with artistic despair. The three men leaped to their feet.

"I'll see to this matter. Stand clear," Colonel Mustard said with much authority.

"I'll accompany you, to minister to the departed's soul," Mr. Green said.

"Oh, I say," Professor Plum said.

The three of them trooped away.

Mrs. Peacock pushed away her soup and reached for the bread and butter. "Eat up, Josephine. It will be a long time until dinner."

Several hours later Mrs. Peacock ensconced herself on the chaise lounge in the conservatory with the daily paper. The lounge was still cordoned off. Professor Plum wandered in before she'd finished reading the first page. Oh, dear. More mandatory small talk with an unresponsive companion.

"I've brought the crossword, Mrs. Peacock. Do you like crosswords?" he asked.

She almost grinned at him. A man working a puzzle is a man who does not expect conversation. "I'm sure you find them most rewarding."

He settled onto the bench seat and spread his paper on his lap. Mrs. Peacock returned to her paper, leafing through until she found an item describing Coco Chanel's latest show.

"I say, Mrs. Peacock, I'd, um, like to talk to Miss Scarlet but I don't know what to say."

How a man could get to be approaching forty and not know the rudiments of speaking to ladies was beyond her. "Josephine likes to do the talking. You only need to ask her a question, and she'll talk to you for hours. Try asking her about her latest play."

"I say, that is wizard. Thank you." He buried his nose in his crossword.

The door was flung open, setting up a draught that shivered the orchid leaves.

"This it just too tedious, with the lounge roped off." Miss Scarlet flounced into the conservatory in a strapless vermillion gown that rippled over her hips. "The colonel and the reverend are playing billiards. Too boring. Is there anything interesting happening in here?"

"Not yet," Mrs. Peacock said, "But give it a few minutes and perhaps something will crop up."

Professor Plum looked up, bewildered, as Miss Scarlet dropped into a chair with a theatrical sigh. Mrs. Peacock gave him the nod. She would have given him a prod if she'd been closer.

"I say, Miss Scarlet, I, er, was wondering, er, how you got started in acting?"

"How kind of you to ask, Professor. It was about ten years ago, after I left school. I met a young man named Jet Midnight. He had a traveling theatrical company called Midnight Smoke. They had a tour going of pastiches and musicals. They needed an ingénue, and I was perfect. So I joined them, and we had such fun, doing the college circuit, living in caravans, working on a different stage every night, playing to a different audience. There were just a few actors, and lots of stage managers, props people, lighting people, and the like. I had a stage name, too. Ruby Raven. They gave me a colossal red wig to wear. I thought my own brown hair was so much more attractive but they said the synthetic red glowed under the lights and made my skin sparkle. All the actors wore wigs. We had such good times. I remember the night when. . . ."

Mrs. Peacock tuned her out and returned to her newspaper. Fifteen minutes later, she glanced up. Professor Plum's pencil lay on the bench, and only one word filled the blanks of his puzzle. Her daughter was waving her arms in the air, recounting another of her triumphs, no doubt.

"And I just couldn't believe it, with four people in charge of props, and six handling the lighting, that the cushion I was to run my finger along at that line was not there. I mean, it just wasn't there. It wasn't merely in the wrong place, it was absent. And there was only one spotlight on me when there should have been two, to give me sufficient backlighting, and so I stopped right there and gave the stage crew what for."

"Really? Then what happened?" Professor Plum seemed on the edge of his seat with enthrallment. Either that, or his backside had grown numb on the bench.

"There was a hush over the audience. I could feel it. So I spoke right up. I had them hanging on my every word. Hardly anyone coughed.

Some silly soul pulled the wrong cord and the curtain came down. I let him have a piece of my mind, let me tell you. I could hear my voice ringing off the rafters. It does that, when I use my voice techniques properly. I told him to get that curtain back up, I was in the middle of a speech, and we had two more acts to go. He fumbled and fumbled, and by the time he'd found the right rope and raised the curtain again, the audience was gone. They'd all mistook it for the end of the play and left."

"Really? Then what happened?"

"Well, the prop person and the lighting person were really angry, shouting at me like it was all my fault the curtain fell down. They said I'd ruined the whole set-up, but really, if anyone ruined the set, it was that wretched prop person who lost the cushion. The next thing I knew, I stood alone on the stage."

"Really? Then what happened?"

"I took off my costume and wig, put on my street clothes, and went back to the caravans to give Jet a piece of my mind about his slovenly stage crew. There was no one there. I was so angry I packed my suitcase and walked toward the closest hotel to get a room and call Mother to wire me some money. I was not going to stand for poor stage management holding back my career. Then the strangest thing happened."

"Really?"

"Jet came running by, sprinting actually. He saw me on the sidewalk and thrust a black bundle at me as he was running. He didn't stop, or explain, or anything. I carried on to the hotel anyway. Let him come and apologize in person if he wanted me back. I had been humiliated, and he would have to grovel. He didn't come the next day. I waited a second day, but there was no sign of him. I wrapped his gift in tissue, packed it in my suitcase, and got on a train to Mother's. Jet's gift was all I had as payment for two week's work. I may have to sell it soon if Mother remains less than generous. I hope it's worth something."

"Really? Then what happened?"

"I'm thirsty. I must protect my vocal cords. I wonder if Mrs. White would make some coffee." She left, walking in the direction of the kitchen.

Professor Plum stared after her, his mouth hanging open.

"You did very well, Professor. You see, as I told you, Josephine will do all the talking if you get her started. If she doesn't return, you'll be able to get on with your crossword knowing you opened the door to friendship."

"No, I say, really, this is quite astonishing."

"What is?"

"Her story. It quite reminds me of an episode at Oxford several years ago. There was a traveling theatre troupe putting on a play, I can't remember the names. I didn't go; I had papers to mark that night. I heard afterward that the play was quite dreadful, the lead character was hopeless, and at the end of Act One she threw a tantrum on stage. Mercifully, the curtains came down and the audience escaped. Do you think it was the same event? It couldn't have been. Miss Scarlet is, I'm sure, a fine actress."

"Quite." What could she say? Professor Plum had all the markings of a suitor, and a married Josephine would be less likely to pester her for money every second day.

"I'd forgotten all about the play," Plum continued. "That same evening there was an uproar around the residences. A gang of common thieves had broken in and stolen all the silver and other valuables from every room. The police chased them down. Most of the stolen goods were recovered, but a few items remained missing. Most of the gang were captured and put in jail. Last I heard the police were still looking for the ringleader and a couple of missing accomplices. The front men, they called them. People who created a distraction while the thieves did their work. Apparently there'd been a string of such robberies in several cities. They were only caught this time because the front men botched up their job. People who had been out for the evening came home early and caught the thieves red-handed."

Miss Scarlet flounced back in. "No coffee. There's never coffee when you need it."

"I thought you all might enjoy a cup of tea, seeing as we've been in a bit of an upset today," Mrs. White said, following Miss Scarlet into the room. She plunked a full tray on the lid of the fish tank, sending all the calico ryukins darting for the bottom.

"Did someone say tea?" Mr. Green asked from the doorway. "Mustard and I are quite parched. Blessed are those who thirst."

There was a flurry of activity around the tea tray, and a scramble for the best seats. Mrs. Peacock found herself perched on the edge of the stone fountain balancing her teacup on her lap.

"I don't suppose we'll find out who killed Master Boddy," Mrs. White said, pouring the final cup. "The policemen seem to be perplexed about it."

Mrs. Peacock cleared her throat. "They might be, but I know who did it. I accuse you of killing Boddy in the lounge with the lead pipe."

Clocked

Solution:

Teacups hung suspended betwixt saucers and lips.

"Who?" Plum asked.

"Josephine, of course," Mrs. Peacock said. "She had Boddy's Coalport clock. She had it wrapped in tissue in her room. Boddy searched her luggage and found it."

"All right, someone did search my luggage and take my clock." Miss Scarlet frowned. "Who says it belonged to John? It could have been anybody's clock."

"It belonged to Sir Hugh and then to John Boddy." Mrs. Peacock took off her hat and produced the photograph. "This photograph shows Boddy ready to go to boarding school. He must have been eight or ten years old. The clock is plainly visible on the mantel behind him. He had this photograph in the lounge this morning. He was showing it to you, to prove the clock belonged to him. I expect he took the clock with him to school when he was older."

"He did, right enough," Mrs. White said. "He was promoted to don, you see, and had his own suite. It had to look proper done up like. He pinched that clock from right under my nose, he did. I was right pressed to find something else suitable to put on the lounge mantel in its place. I hate people moving the whatnots around."

Mrs. Peacock refreshed her tea. "So Josephine got an acting job with a group which had too few actors and too many crew. When the theatrical troupe put on plays, drawing in the local college people, most of the crew were robbing the houses of the audience. This particular night they were in Oxford when the lead actress messed up the play and it closed early. The audience went home and caught the pseudo-troupe members nicking the silver."

"I didn't mess it up. I gave the stagehands a dressing down."

"On the stage right in the middle of Act One. That's a bit of a deviation from the script. You messed up the play, my dear."

Green nodded. "Rather sounds that way."

"As I was saying, the theatrical troupe was a front for a gang of thieves," Mrs. Peacock continued. "They only put on plays to lure people out of their houses. When Mr. Midnight ran past you and tossed you a bundle, he wasn't giving you a gift. He was getting rid of the evidence. That evidence came to light today when Mr. Boddy found the clock in your room."

Miss Scarlet dangled a hand to her forehead. "I had no idea Jet Midnight was up to such shenanigans. I did wonder why the backstage crew was so large, yet there were never any of them around when you needed them. Jet said they worked shifts, so they wouldn't get tired carrying all those papier mâché sets around."

"So what happened to Boddy?" Professor Plum asked.

"Mrs. White came in to the lounge with the clock and put it back on the mantel. Green came in, mumbled a few words, poured himself some of that wretched cold coffee, put it down, and left. Mrs. White said something and left."

"As I thought. You didn't stop shouting long enough to hear what I said." Green sniffed.

"John came into the lounge carrying a fresh coffee tray. He poured himself a cup. He said something, which I didn't hear. He threw his entire cup at me. I was stupefied. My gown was dripping."

"But he gained himself some silence." Mrs. Peacock nodded. She'd remember that for Josephine's next tantrum. Throw water at her.

"He said I had stolen his clock, and I was going to go to jail for it, just like all my nasty friends. Between the lack of decent coffee, his accusation, and his dousing me, I was speechless with anger. I grabbed the lead pipe from the tray and whacked him with it. He fell into the chair, I think, but I really wasn't paying attention to him. He'd drenched me in hot coffee. I had to run and get changed."

"Well I never, pinching the Coalport clock. Where's that clock now, that's what I'd like to know," Mrs. White said.

Mrs. Peacock thought about the struggle she'd have trying to reassemble the clock. "I expect the police will take it with them as evidence. You may not get it back."

Rock of Ages

Colonel Mustard slipped quietly out the rear door near the conservatory, into the kitchen garden. Oops, wrong location. He crept along the pathways until he passed the compost heap and emerged in a little copse of woods sloping gently upwards over a knoll. He followed an overgrown stone pathway past several trees, and came upon a granite monument, half choked in weeds. Very interesting, but he was on a mission.

A little further on he found a loose stone in the path. He glanced back over his shoulder. From this vantage point, he couldn't be seen from the house.

Perfect.

He overturned the stone and scraped away a little of the dirt with the toe of his boot until he had a bowl-sized hollow. He upturned the dish in his hands, consigning its contents to the earth. Grosset Fool, Mrs. White called it. A man would be a fool to eat it. His mother had made it when the gooseberry bushes were laden, and it no more resembled this atrocity than mutton-resembled spinach.

He tamped the stone back in place with his riding crop. There. May the insects eat it and die quickly. Now on to Part Two of the mission, to return undetected.

Fortunately, when he reached the dining room, Miss Scarlet had created a diversion, spilling her Fool on the carpet. Mrs. White was down on her hands and knees, muttering and dabbing with a rag.

Mr. Green was taking advantage of the moment, tiptoeing into the kitchen with his bowl. Professor Plum was staring around in indecisive panic, his Fool untouched before him. Mrs. Peacock had attempted to eat the concoction, and leaned back in her seat looking pale.

"What's this then?" Colonel Mustard asked, a little too loudly.

Professor Plum jumped, his elbow jostling his bowl. Colonel Mustard finished the job for him with his riding crop, flipping the bowl upside-down on the table.

"What ho, dreadfully sorry, old chap, most clumsy of me."

"Oh, dear, what a mess, I shall help clean it up, entirely my fault." Professor Plum stammered his way through a string of apologies all the way to the kitchen, although he looked relieved.

Placing his empty bowl at his place, Colonel Mustard turned his attention to Mrs. Peacock, who was looking grayer by the minute. "Dear lady, I feel you need a little fresh air to clear your sinuses. The aroma from the Fool is a little heady, all that cinnamon and cayenne. A turn in the garden would be just the ticket."

He marched to her place at the table, grasped her elbow, lifted her onto her feet, and propelled her out the door. She went along unresisting with wobbly knees. He hurried her past the kitchen garden into the copse and up the path.

"There, a nice secluded spot, just the ticket. I'll stand guard back along the path." He left her leaning on a tree and trotted back a distance until he was in sight of the mansion. He took up sentry duty there, standing at ease, facing the mansion, his back to Mrs. Peacock. Privacy. Sometimes a man, or woman, needs a few minutes alone.

He heard retching noises, then silence. He waited a few more minutes. Give a bloke a chance to sort himself out. Or herself, in this case.

On his return up the path, he found Mrs. Peacock perched on a granite block looking pale but pinker.

"Lovely day for a stroll in the woods, what ho," he said, swinging his riding crop at some tall weeds encroaching the path. "I intended to come up here after lunch, to examine the granite statue I noticed earlier. You seem to have located another one. Are you feeling up to a field trip?"

"Yes, I'm much better now, thank you. Fresh air was all I needed. I'm sure that woman made one of her hideous substitutions in that Fool. Do you think this is a statue? I thought this was a tall seat." Mrs. Peacock stood up and examined her perch. "Oh, it looks like a giant head."

Colonel Mustard swung his riding crop around the base to clear away the weeds. "Granite, I'd say. Lovely smooth forehead to sit on. Winged headdress and tubular beard indicate it's Egyptian. Seen a number of this type. One of the Pharaohs, I should say."

"Do you think it's authentic?"

"I shouldn't like to guess. We'll ask Plum. He's the expert."

"I can't imagine it's the real thing. Who'd leave an Egyptian sculpture out in the woods to grow moss?"

"Oh, there's more than one. Follow me."

Colonel Mustard trudged down the path and pointed out the monument he had first seen on his original mission. "See there? An obelisk. As tall as you. Looks like it's been broken into sections and patched together. Some writing on it. We'll need to get Plum to translate."

Mrs. Peacock ran her fingers down the smooth granite. "This little path leads from one to the other. Do you suppose Sir Hugh was building a statue garden? It would be most delightful to sit here this summer, in the shade. Such a shame it's all overgrown. We ought to get a work party organized. Get the others to come out and we'll all cut down weeds."

"Say no more, say no more. Done a spot of organizing the troops in my time. I'll have a work detail organized in a trice. Shouldn't wonder they'll all be grateful for a spot of fresh air after that lunch debacle."

Within the half-hour Colonel Mustard stood at the head of the path handing out an assortment of knives to the others. Mrs. White slashed at the weeds and shrubbery with a huge knife wielded with vengeance. Miss Scarlet poked her knife at the daisies and took frequent rests on the giant-head statue. Professor Plum worked like an archaeologist, inching along the path, chopping grass blade by blade with a tiny knife more suitable for cutting fruit. Mr. Green veered away from the paths, cutting tunnels to nowhere with a machete. Mrs. Peacock remained focussed on her mission, clearing a path to the giant-head bench. Mustard was well pleased with the work, as he watched it progress. The little stone pathway rose from the undergrowth like a magic carpet. He took care to remain standing on the stone he had previously visited with his Fool.

"Are you not going to do anything but watch us work?" Mrs. White asked, pointing her knife at him.

"I'm the commanding officer. I am working. It's my duty to see that the work progresses on schedule."

"Schedule? I'll show you a schedule. Teatime, that's a schedule, and you'll all be right miffed if I don't produce a tray of scones and tea after this work. So I'll be off." Mrs. White wiped her hands on her apron and marched away to the kitchen, knife in hand.

"Oh, look," Miss Scarlet squealed from her granite perch. "I think I see another one. It's as tall as you, Colonel Mustard."

Professor Plum stood up and hurried to her side, his bow tie askew.

"Where? Oh, there. Yes, it's life size, as tall as I am. Why, I believe I know that one. Oh, I say." He plunged toward it, hacking greenery as he went.

Miss Scarlet followed him, kicking the fallen weeds out of the way with her red sandals.

Mr. Green paused for a moment on the bench. Mrs. Peacock considered joining the others, then resumed her work on a path leading to an oak tree.

"What do you think, old boy," Mustard asked Green. "Do you think they're the genuine article?"

"More like plaster lawn ornaments. I think I'll go and see if that tea's anywhere near ready." He tucked his machete under his arm and wandered toward the mansion.

"Come along, Mother, this is too precious for words," Miss Scarlet shouted.

Mustard joined the remaining work detail at the new discovery site.

"He's just lovely, a whole statue, seated on his own stone bench, with a face and everything," Miss Scarlet gushed. "Look, Colonel, he's all there. I could sit on his knee. He's got that same funny hat on, and the same beard. Do you suppose it's the same fellow?"

Plum raked his hands through his hair. "No, this is Sobekemzaf I. See, there's his name, right there." He pointed to a row of hieroglyphics. "That other one, the one you were sitting on, is Amenemhat III. The obelisk belonged to Hatshepsut, although we'll probably find her name has been scratched off. They did that, erased her name."

"Why? Didn't they like her?" Miss Scarlet asked.

Professor Plum didn't answer. He stared at the seated figure, then looked back at the others. "I wonder if there's a fourth."

"Fourth what?"

"Fourth statue. Limestone. Queen Ahmose-Merytamun. Upper torso. Too tall to sit on."

Miss Scarlet clapped her hands. "Oh, goody, a treasure hunt. Let's get slashing. Should we follow the path left or right? Colonel, we'd find it sooner if you got a knife and did some real work."

"She's quite right, Colonel, and we seem to be losing our workforce." Mrs. Peacock raised an eyebrow at him.

"Indeed. I shall avail myself of a tool and set to."

Colonel Mustard wandered down the path to the garden potting shed and rummaged around until he found a suitable knife, not too big, not too small, with a decent heft. By the time he returned, the work party had found the missing sculpture.

"Look at her big hair," Miss Scarlet said. "She has big ears, too, but at least she doesn't have a beard. This is only her upper body. Where's the rest of her?"

"Back in Karnack. Sometimes when you find these things they've been broken. Vandals, or poachers, or earthquakes. The usual." Plum shook his head and his bow tie wobbled. "I don't understand."

"You seem distressed, Professor," Mrs. Peacock said. "Do come and sit on the giant head and tell us all about it."

Plum allowed himself to be led along the path to Amenemhat's head. "This is one of two. They would be complete statues flanking the door of the temple of the cat goddess Bastet. I couldn't get the other one, the Egyptians insisted on keeping it."

"What are you babbling about?" Mrs. Peacock demanded.

Plum let out a deep sigh. "I was on a dig in Egypt. Sir Hugh and I had an arrangement. He funded my summer digs while I taught at Oxford. I sent him some small artifacts each season. You may have noticed them on the mantel in the lounge. After he died the funding continued. I dug up this granite head eight years ago and shipped it back to England. Not to this estate, to the British Museum. I thought if they saw a sample of my work, they'd hire me. Teaching is so tedious. I didn't hear from them. They never received this object. It was sent here to Tudor Hall instead. I don't understand."

"Buck up, man. Even your bow tie is drooping," Colonel Mustard commanded. He hated to see despondency in the troops. Bad for the morale. "We'll get to the bottom of this. Make it our mission. Now then, did you do your own digging?"

"Yes, me and my crew. I was there every day, watching. I saw them hoist it on the truck."

"Then what?"

"Then I went into Cairo with the truck and arranged for shipping. Verdant Import Export. They do a dandy job of packing crates."

"So you can vouch for it up until you handed it over for shipping."

"Right."

"You look most dejected," Mrs. Peacock said. "Josephine, run to the kitchen and get Mrs. White to make some tea. Bring it out here. There's a dear."

"Why me?" Miss Scarlet whined.

"Because your heels are less spiky than mine. And while you're waiting for the kettle to boil, ask Boddy where he got these statues."

Miss Scarlet returned in ten minutes with a tray of tea. "Boddy says he bought them from Jade Collectibles. They have a catalogue. He thought they'd make a nice ornamental garden. He says Mrs. White hasn't been keeping up with the weeding. Mrs. White says she does the work of three people but is only paid for one. They're having a row."

"Oh, dear," Mrs. Peacock said. "Dinner will be spoiled."

"Perhaps she'll only feel up to making chips and egg. That would be a bit of all right." Mustard felt his stomach rumbling at the thought of a chip butty.

Plum took his teacup and moped around the four statues. Mustard couldn't think of anything to say to cheer him up. All he could think about was bringing a deck chair up here so he could sit and enjoy the cool of the woods.

A moment later Plum put his cup down on the tray and pulled a magnifying glass and a little whisk from his pocket. He began mincing around the statues, whisking and examining them.

"Whatever are you looking for?" Mrs. Peacock asked. "A rare strain of moss?"

"You didn't tell us about the other three statues," Miss Scarlet said. "I'm killed with curiosity about them. Tell us about the one with big hair."

Plum straightened up. "That's a Hathor wig. The goddess Hathor wore her hair in that style. Queen Ahmose-Merytamun, that's who that is. The rest of her is back in Karnak. The next year I went back to Karnak and found him." He pointed to the seated figure. "Sobekemzaf I. His eye sockets are empty but he would have had inlaid eyes. Someone stole them centuries ago. You can see by the marks around the gaps that someone struggled to pry them out."

"What about that pointy thing?"

"The obelisk of Hatshepsut. I found it in three pieces. Someone had broken it up and used it to build another structure. It's a solar symbol, sacred to the gods of the sun."

"And you shipped these all home?" Mustard asked.

"Yes, through Verdant to the British Museum. I really don't understand what they're doing here." He bent to his whisking and peering task.

The others finished their tea and piled the cups on the tray.

"It's peaceful here. I wonder if the row is finished. I should like to get a book and bring it up here to read." Mrs. Peacock leaned on the giant head.

Plum stood up, put his tools on the giant head and straightened his bow tie. "I'm going to have a word with Boddy." He strode off down the path with more gumption than Mustard had ever seen in him.

"I'm thinking about seeking out some deck chairs, making a little spot up here. With a little more clipping back of the grass, it would be serviceable." Mustard pointed around with his riding crop.

"We could bring a blanket and have a picnic up here," Miss Scarlet suggested.

"That would be considerably more convenient when Mrs. White serves one of her aberrations," Mrs. Peacock said. "It would eliminate the sneaking out into the garden with a full plate." She raised an eyebrow at Mustard.

He cleared his throat. He was sure no one had seen him.

"Do you think we could have a picnic here tomorrow?" Miss Scarlet asked. "I wonder if I could persuade Mrs. White to pack a basket."

"You might be able to persuade her if you put her in a good mood first by returning the tea tray to the kitchen." Mrs. Peacock straightened up. "It must be almost dinner time. I wonder why the gong hasn't rung."

Mustard escorted the ladies back down the slope to the house. He allowed Miss Scarlet to carry the tray, since he needed one hand on his riding crop to brush errant weeds from their route.

They found the kitchen deserted. No pots rumbled on the Aga

cooker. Evidence of foraging lay on the counter, in the form of an empty tin of salmon, with a trail of crumbs leading to the dining room.

Miss Scarlet placed the tea tray beside the sink. "I'm sure Mrs. White will look after this later. What will we do for dinner? Can you cook us something, Mother?"

"My dear Josephine, I discuss cooking. I don't do cooking. I think I'll have a piece of toast."

"Need something heartier myself," Mustard said. "Think I'll pop down to the local in the village. Fancy a haddock and chips."

"I'll come with you," Miss Scarlet said. "I can't even think about cooking something in this kitchen. It's too big."

An hour later Mustard reveled in a hot plate of fish and chips, with thick slabs of homemade bread to make a chip butty. He felt like he hadn't eaten for days. Just like at the siege of Khartoum. Miss Scarlet seemed to find the young local lads quite interesting, so he didn't have to have his meal ruined by listening to her twaddle.

When they returned to the mansion, they found lights on in every room, and everyone in a state of panic.

Mrs. Peacock met them at the door. "Thank goodness you're back. Mr. Boddy's been murdered. Stabbed. Colonel, you must take charge. No one seems to be able to accomplish anything constructive."

Mustard straightened his uniform. "Lead the way, dear lady."

Mrs. Peacock took him to the conservatory.

Mr. Boddy lay on the floor near the windows, a pair of binoculars around his neck and a tiny knife in his back.

"Rather a large hole for such a tiny knife," Miss Scarlet said, behind him.

"Stand clear, ladies," Mustard said. "I shall take charge of the situation. Has anyone rung for the police?"

"No," Mrs. Peacock said. "I could do that now, if you like."

"Please do. Then settle yourselves in the lounge. It will be a tedious evening, I'm afraid."

He shut the door as they left.

He examined the body carefully. As Miss Scarlet had said, the hole was rather large but the little knife stood up proudly in it. Boddy must have been bird watching at the windows, glimpsing the sparrows as they flittered in the copse of trees on the knoll.

Beside Boddy on the floor he found a little whisk and a magnifying glass. That seemed to be everything. He sat down to await the authorities. On the table he found a catalogue for Jade Imports. He picked it up and flipped through it while he waited. Jolly interesting. Lots of whatnots and doodads from India, Africa, and the Continent. He tucked it under his arm and took it with him when the police arrived.

The next day after elevenses, Mustard took the catalogue and went in search of a deck chair. He found one in the drive shed near a stack of kindling. The kindling consisted of broken tree boughs and chopped up packing crates. He could read words on the top flat bit. *DANT SHIP.* The remains of a boat that wouldn't float, he suspected. With chair in hand he marched up the knoll and settled into a shady spot in the sculpture garden.

Shortly thereafter his peace was disturbed by a troop carrying a basket and chairs.

"Look, we've brought a picnic lunch," Miss Scarlet said, laughing. "Mrs. White thought it was a capital idea to get out of the house while those nasty policemen tromp around."

Professor Plum helped Miss Scarlet spread out the blanket, while Mr. Green set up the deck chairs. Mrs. White opened the basket and Mrs. Peacock passed out linen napkins.

"What are you reading, Mustard?" Plum asked.

"A catalogue I found in the conservatory. Makes a nice light read on a warm day."

"I'll bet it has pretty pictures," Miss Scarlet said, pulling it from his hands. "Oh, there's a wonderful silver and turquoise necklace. Look, Mother, it's just your style."

Mrs. White passed around a platter of sandwiches. "There's plenty, so eat up. I've made chopped greens to go with them, and lemon tarts for afters."

Mustard helped himself to several sandwiches as the platter passed him. "I hope we won't be inconvenienced too long by the police. The tea gets cold quickly out here."

"We could hurry them along if we found out who did it," Mrs. Peacock said. "Any ideas, Mustard?"

"I do have a theory or two, since I spent some time considering the scene of the crime," he said. He sat up a little straighter and tapped his riding crop into the dirt. "I accuse you of stabbing Mr. Boddy with a knife in the conservatory."

ROCK OF AGES

SOLUTION:

All eyes swiveled.

"Who me?"

"No, him."

"No, her."

Mustard held a hand up. "I mean you, Plum. You were upset about finding your statues here instead of at the British Museum. The knife you were using to cut the shrubbery was found in the body. Your magnifying glass and whisk were found beside the body."

"I say, that's completely mad." Plum flushed violet.

"I'll say," Mrs. White said. "That knife wouldn't cut butter. It couldn't cut through Master Boddy's suit and reach his heart."

"I quite agree with Mustard," Mr. Green said. "I think if he put his mind to it, used a little muscle, Plum could use that knife for the purpose."

"Pish tosh," Mrs. Peacock said. "Any fool can see Mrs. White's right. It was no bigger than this one." She held out a butter knife.

Colonel Mustard studied the little knife. "Correct assumptions. Knife not adequate for the job. Insufficient strength in the blade."

"I say, why would I possibly want to kill Boddy?" Plum asked.

"Because he prevented you from getting the job at the museum. Every year you tried to move on and every year you had to remain teaching. That would drive anyone to murder." Green sampled another sandwich. "These are quite good. What are they?"

"Boiled tongue," Mrs. White said. "One of my favorites."

"I remember I left my magnifying glass and whisk on the big head over there," Plum continued.

"You could have come back and retrieved them at any time," Green said. "We were all over the place last night. I was playing billiards. Mrs. White was in the dining room. Mrs. Peacock was in the lounge. Colonel Mustard and Miss Scarlet were down in the village. No one would have noticed."

"I was in the kitchen making a sandwich," Plum protested. "I took it to the lounge."

"Oh, look," Miss Scarlet said. "Here's the big-head statue in this catalogue. *Authentic. One only.* Isn't that interesting? We're sitting here in front of it, and it's in the catalogue. So's the big hair lady."

"Let me see that." Mrs. White snatched the catalogue from her hands. "They're all here. All four."

"Must be an old catalogue," Green said. "Printed before Boddy bought them."

"1926. This year. And how would they get into Jade Collectibles catalogue when I shipped them through Verdant Shipping?"

"An interesting point. I think, from the looks of the broken-up packing crates in the drive shed, that Verdant Shipping handles the work for Jade as well as for the professor," Mustard said. "Perhaps they made a shipping error and sent your lot to Boddy instead of the British Museum. So you were angry with him for taking your finds and not returning them, when they were sent in error."

"That doesn't explain how they came to be in Jade's catalogue," Mrs. Peacock said.

"A minor point," Green said. "What matters is that Plum was angry about finding them here, and his tools were found with the body."

"Yes, you were quite cross yesterday when you went to have a word with Boddy." Miss Scarlet said.

"I didn't do it. Somebody is trying to frame me." Plum stammered. "Mrs. White and Mr. Boddy had a row."

"Mrs. White didn't see your tools. She had already gone back to the house. How would she know to put them at the scene?" Mustard asked. "Admit it, my boy. The jig is up. You killed Boddy for stealing your statues."

Plum sputtered and stared around. All eyes were on him. Mustard braced himself for action in case the man tried to make a run for it.

"There would be no reason for that," Plum said in a calm voice. "Those statues are fakes."

"No!"

"Really?"

"Well I never heard tell."

"Yes, it's true." Plum straightened his bow tie. "They're supposed to be granite. They're plaster of Paris and grey paint. I told Boddy so yesterday. Told him he had been duped, as I had been duped. We'd been victims of a scam. We agreed to get to the bottom of it. Boddy showed me the catalogue of Jade Imports. He said he had ordered the statues, one a year, to make a sculpture garden. He'd paid dearly for them, believing they were original Egyptian artifacts. They'd arrived via Verdant Shipping. He'd had the men carry them up the hill, so he hadn't taken a close look. When he hired the local men to construct the path, the statues were getting mossy, so they looked quite authentic. He had no reason to suspect otherwise."

"So what happened?" Miss Scarlet asked. "I'm not quite following this."

"I entrusted my finds to Verdant Shipping. They made plaster copies and put them for sale in the Jade Collectibles catalogue. So Verdant and Jade must be the same company."

"Well, where are the real ones, then?"

"Sold to the highest bidder, I should expect," Mrs. Peacock said. "So all we need to know now is, who's behind those two companies?"

Miss Scarlet smiled. "I don't know, but look, here's a photo of the president of Jade. *A Few Words from Our President.* It looks rather like you, Mr.Green, only this man has a moustache and beard."

Mustard grabbed the catalogue. "Why I believe she's right. This is you, Green, in a disguise. You have been running a business in counterfeit collectibles."

Green jumped to his feet. "You don't really believe that. Look at the evidence. Plum's tools were found with the body. Plum's knife was the murder weapon." He stepped over to the obelisk. "We have only his word for it that these are fakes." He slapped the obelisk hard with the palm of his hand. "Granite. This is granite."

The obelisk cracked in half and fell over, exposing a crumbly white interior.

The Wheels of Coffee Grind Slow

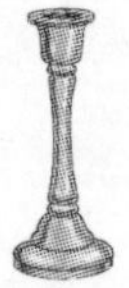

"Mrs. White, whatever are you doing?"

"Grinding coffee for elevenses."

Mr. Green watched her whacking a paper bag with a lead pipe. He raised his eyes and scanned the counter. In the corner he spotted an iron mechanical coffee grinder with a wind-up handle. It was shaped like a little pot-bellied stove, with a lid on the top for pouring in the beans and a drawer at the bottom for taking out the ground coffee. "You have a coffee grinder over there. Why not use it? Surely that would be easier than brute strength."

"I don't like to use that. It might wear out, and then where would I be? And I'd have to clean it afterwards, and it's all intricate parts, difficult to get a dishcloth into. This does just as well. The pieces are a bit uneven, but it's only coffee."

Green sighed. Only coffee. Nectar of the Gods, when he'd first tasted it in America at the seminary. Robust and hearty, nutty and smooth. Only Miss Scarlet and he understood coffee, how it should taste, why you would want to drink it several times a day. Someday soon, he'd need to go back to America and restore his soul over a dark aromatic cup, hot and sweet, with cream.

"But surely it would result in a more even grind if you used the machine."

"Mayhap, but does it matter? This lead pipe does the job. And besides, last time I put coffee beans in that grinder, it jammed up, so it isn't working anyway."

Visions of perfect full-bodied coffee danced through his mind. If he could fix the coffee grinder, volunteer to grind some beans with it, he might be rewarded with a sturdy compelling brew with a hint of smokiness and a distinct nuance, or a buttery creamy sweet blend with the lingering essence of vanilla and nuts. Coffee, real coffee.

"Let me have a look at that grinder," he said. "I might be able to unblock it for you. Then I would grind a test lot to make sure it's functioning."

"If you've a mind to, go ahead. This method works just as well, in my opinion." She gave her paper bag a hard whack with the lead pipe and the bag burst, scattering coffee bean shards all over the counter. "Except when that happens. I hate messes." She laid down her lead pipe and used a dingy dishcloth to swipe all the coffee bits into a pot of water. She put this pot on the Aga cooker and left it to heat through. "That's that, then. Coffee will be ready on time. I'll be off into the garden now to pick some veg for lunch."

No wonder the coffee tasted like dishwater. Mrs. White had no idea how finely the coffee needed to be ground, and obviously took no great care with its preparation. He'd be lucky not to find bits of rhubarb leaves or toast crumbs in his cup. He picked up the coffee grinder and took it into the dining room where he could work at it without her hanging over his shoulder telling him the coffee was perfectly serviceable as it was.

It was a simple mechanical machine. A chute for the beans. A system of grinding wheels and augers that fed the beans through several steps of grinding until they had reached a powder-like consistency. A small drawer to collect the ground coffee. One pulled out the drawer and poured the contents into a coffee percolator. He'd lay odds there was such a device somewhere in the kitchen, gathering dust. John Boddy had been born in America. His parents would have drunk coffee, and when they disappeared their household goods would have been sent here with the boy.

He found a sharp knife in the Welsh dresser and began taking the grinder apart. He heard footsteps in the kitchen, and hoped Mrs. White wasn't going to serve her imitation coffee immediately. If he had half an hour, he might be able to produce some first-rate coffee. A sweet and perfumy blend with a hint of roasted almonds. Or a spicy burnt caramel cup with an overlay of cedar and chocolate. Whatever magic these beans held, he could release it, he was sure.

The mechanism seemed to be jammed. He peered into the dark little chamber as he tried turning the hand crank. Something hard was solidly blocking the wheels. He jabbed at it with the knife. Sometimes when you bought peppercorns from a peddler there were a few black stones in the bag to fill it out. Perhaps someone was adding stones to the coffee beans to tip the scales.

After five minutes of persistent poking, tapping, and wiggling the handle, the grinder remained firmly jammed. In desperation, he turned the grinder upside down and rapped it hard on the floor. It took several firm smacks, and a dent or two in the hardwood, but he managed to dislodge the offending greasy stone. He pushed it to one side and tested the grinder's handle. It turned as smoothly as the arm on a counterfeit engraving press.

Success. He could almost taste the coffee now. Peachy overtones on a buttery base. If he hurried into the kitchen for fresh beans, he could empty the pot on the Aga cooker, and start anew. He scooped the grinder into his arms.

The gong announced elevenses.

Too late.

The dining room door swished open behind him. "Mr. Green!"

"Yes, Mrs. White? See, I've fixed it."

"What's all this, then?" Mrs. White asked, balancing the coffee tray on the table edge. "What's this crumbs on the table?"

"That's grinds from the coffee grinder. I managed to free it. It works now." He picked up the stone and rolled it in his fingers, rubbing the coffee residue off. "It had this pebble stuck in it."

"Right, then. As I expected. Someone was trying to dun us with that sack of coffee. I've found such a pile of pebbles in it. I've had to sieve them out before I ground the coffee. If I'm not careful, they bite right through my paper bag, and then I've a mess to clean up. Just like this morning."

Mr. Green looked down at the offending pebble. Without the coffee coating it, it was vaguely milky colored, no, translucent and very, very hard. "You say you've found a lot of these?"

"Yes, one or two every day, nearly."

"What do you do with them?"

"Tip them on the compost pile with the other coffee grinds. Or, if they come out in my sieve, toss them in the fish tank. Sometimes I find them at the bottom of the pot. They're a little cleaner then, so I toss them in the fish tank, too. You can never have too much fresh gravel in a fish tank. It covers up the mess the fish make."

Thoughts of gloriously sublime coffee vanished from Green's mind.

In his fingers he was holding, he was absolutely positive, an uncut diamond.

He slipped it into his suit pocket.

“I’ll be off to the lounge, then, for coffee,” he said with as much calm as he could muster.

“Not until you’ve cleaned up this mess you made. Here’s a duster.”

She produced a dust cloth from her apron. He dutifully swept up the coffee grinds into his palm and carried them to the back door, where he tossed them into the rose bushes. Mrs. White, watching him from the dining room door, seemed mollified.

He returned and picked up the grinder. “I’ll be putting this back, then, and perhaps tomorrow I’ll make the coffee using it.”

She nodded and picked up her tray, heading for the lounge. When the door had closed behind her, he sprinted back through the kitchen, down the passageway through the ballroom to the conservatory.

The fish were spinning madly around the tank, darting around the seaweed, under the china bridge, and past the tiny castle. The gravel floor was heaped up at the edges, like a tornado had passed through and spun it away from the vortex.

Green found the source of the tornado on the tiled floor in front of the fish tank. Mr. Boddy lay there, his sleeves wet to the armpits and a dented curve in one temple that matched the lead pipe lying on the floor. The floor was littered with aquarium gravel.

This was a sad turn of events. He’d have to search Boddy’s pockets for the diamonds. He had no idea how many there might be. Still, it was a methodical job, not difficult. He stuffed his hands into the two outer suit pockets and felt bits of gravel. Boddy had scooped up the diamonds and simply stuffed them into the handiest pockets. Turning them inside out revealed no diamonds. Someone else had collected them. The same someone else who had wielded the lead pipe. If he found the person who had killed Boddy, he’d have found the diamonds. He turned the pockets inside right.

He peeked into the passageway. The coast was clear. He slipped back through the ballroom to the dining room and approached the lounge along this route. No one would know he'd been in the conservatory. He'd find out who had wet cuffs, or gritty fingers, and he'd know who had the diamonds.

The lounge was in consternation. Mrs. White was loudly lamenting the cups and saucers. The silver coffee tray and all its attendant parts were upended on the Oriental rug. Every one of the potential coffee drinkers dabbed at wet sleeves, wet dresses, wet jackets. Three of them scrambled about on hands and knees rescuing shortbread.

"Oh, dear, I've chipped my nails," Miss Scarlet said.

"My dress is ruined." Mrs. Peacock said, pointing to the large wet mark on her blue linen. "How could you be so clumsy?"

"Weren't my fault," Mrs. White said. "People in my way. Look at the state of my china cups, and my apron."

"Does this mean we'll have to do without coffee this morning?" Miss Scarlet stared at the crumpled shortbread in her hands and the sopping sleeves of her kimono.

"Do without coffee? Is that all you can think of? Look at my uniform! This is an outrage." Colonel Mustard held up his arms, both dripping.

Plum shook his head sadly. "I've only the one jacket, you know. I shall have to rinse it out and hang it to dry." He fingered his tweeds.

Green's heart sank. No quick solution presented itself in the reclamation of the diamonds. However, a little silver lining shone through. "I see you're all busy with this unfortunate incident. The Lord helps those. I'll get started on a fresh pot of coffee while Mrs. White finds us more cups. By the time you're all changed, I'll have a treat for you."

He tore back to the kitchen. Coffee, coffee, freshly ground aromatic imported coffee. Rich dark full-bodied flavor with a lingering aftertaste. He grabbed the coffee grinder and opened cupboard doors until he found a percolator. Now all he needed was coffee beans. There, beside the sink, a paper bag. Yes, a half a pound of beans, if he wasn't mistaken. He scattered them on his palm, a handful at a time, checking for pebble-like pieces before he poured them into the grinder. He wasn't sure which was more exciting, hearing the soft whooshing of coffee beans properly ground, or finding two suspect pebbles in the beans.

He set the coffee percolator on the Aga cooker before he dared look at his find. Yes, they looked like diamonds. Where would they have come from? Africa, the origin of most diamonds imported to England. By Mrs. White's account, they were hidden in a sack of coffee.

He rolled the stones in his palm like coins from a collection plate, full of promise. He wondered why they had arrived here in the coffee. He and Boddy had run a few illegal operations in the last few years after Sir Hugh died and left some profitable ventures without a front man. Someone in this mansion must be working on a shady deal with Boddy. Boddy was collaborating with another scoundrel like himself. Perhaps the heady mixture had arrived several days ago, and Mrs. White had not thought to mention it, just begun using the coffee. Boddy would have been frantic when he discovered his diamonds had been pressed into service as aquarium gravel. So would the person who found Boddy dipping for diamonds amongst the fish.

Therefore, to find the person with a pocket full of diamonds, he'd only need to find out who had been in Africa lately in a diamond-producing country. He'd been in Africa himself. He knew diamonds came from South Africa, the Belgian Congo, Angola, Ghana, Guinea, Sierra Leone, and Rhodesia.

The coffee was ready. A smoky hazelnut nose promising a nutty roasted flavor. He carried the percolator in triumph to the lounge. Mrs. White had cleaned up the broken bits of crockery and the only remnant of the accident was a sopping big stain on the Oriental rug. Colonel Mustard was taut in his dress uniform. Plum sat forlorn in his shirt sleeves, his bow tie askew. Mrs. Peacock reigned immaculate, this time in a lightly flowered dress of bluebells, cornflowers and delphiniums. Miss Scarlet wore a simple garnet day dress that clung to her like butter on toast. Her eyes widened when she saw the percolator.

"Do you mean, coffee? Real coffee?" She almost drooled.

"Yes, I mean real coffee, praise the Lord. May I serve you the first cup?"

She snatched a cup and saucer off the tray and proffered it.

He poured.

She sipped. "Oh, in the name of all that's merciful! Real coffee! I shall die of joy!" She retreated into her cup like a nun in search of spiritual solace. "Wait until John tastes this. He'll just die."

"Yes, I'm sure he will," Green said. "Coffee, Mrs. Peacock?"

"Master Boddy asked me about the coffee just this morning," Mrs. White said. "Went off in a tear afterwards."

Green continued to pour coffee, picturing Boddy in a tear all the way to the aquarium to rescue his booty. "I wonder if this is Kenyan coffee. I enjoyed a Kenyan blend while I was in Kenya last year. Hearty with a lingering aftertaste."

Mrs. Peacock sipped. "I think not. It reminds me of coffee they served at the Royal Marampa Hotel in Sierra Leone. Or was it the Hotel Abidjan in the Ivory Coast? One struggles to keep all the places straight. One hotel is much like the other."

"Shouldn't doubt it's an Arabica blend, from Uganda," Colonel

Mustard said. "Enjoyed the odd cup when I was stationed in the Congo. Military intelligence business. All hush-hush, of course, I can say no more about it."

"I say, it reminds me of the Ethiopian Yergacheffe they served in Cairo when I was coming home from a dig in Egypt." Professor Plum sipped and stared at the ceiling. "Or perhaps not. Hard to say. A little fruitier, with overtones of coriander, or is it cloves?"

Miss Scarlet shook her head. "You people are all wrong. It's Harar Longberry, you can tell by the nose. Mother and I had some in the Cape Town Hotel in South Africa."

Green put down the percolator and indulged in his own cup. It was divine, big body, high acidity, rich taste. It erased his disappointment at finding they'd almost all been to diamond-producing countries. He'd have to devise a new plan. Flush the culprit out.

"Where is this particular coffee from, Mrs. White? What does it say on the bag?" he asked.

"I don't know I'm sure. I've enough to do without standing around reading the print on a sack of coffee beans."

"Where might this sack of coffee beans be now, Mrs. White?"

"In the wine cellar. I wasn't having a ruddy great bag of beans cluttering up my kitchen. I scoop some up every day for elevenses."

"Perhaps I can assist you in advance for tomorrow," Green said, draining his cup to the last drop. "I fancy another go at the grinder machine, to make sure it's one hundred percent running order. I'll just go scoop some out and grind it, shall I?"

Mrs. White shrugged, but the hint of a smile played at her lips, as if she was gloating at having fobbed off one of her jobs on an unsuspecting victim.

Green sauntered out of the lounge, scurried down the hall to the kitchen, and slipped through the secret door to the wine cellar. There was the bag of coffee, leaning on the wall behind the Bordeaux. He hid behind the racks of Riesling and waited. It wasn't long before he heard footsteps creaking down the main cellar wooden stairs, creeping along the dim passageway to the wine cellar. As the figure neared the Bordeaux, Green stepped out, startling the intruder.

"I accuse you of killing Mr. Boddy in the conservatory with the lead pipe." Green felt himself glowing with satisfaction at a job well done. Either that or the coffee was making him giddy.

The Wheels of Coffee Grind Slow

Solution:

Colonel Mustard stopped short, his riding crop raised in self-defense. "Oh, it's you."

"Yes, and I think you have been indulging in a little smuggling with Boddy. I think it went wrong somehow and you killed him."

"Never mind that, old chap, I think we can make a deal here."

"A deal?" Green felt his heart quicken. *Deal*. He loved that word.

"I asked Boddy this morning where my share of the profits was. He claimed he didn't have the diamonds, that the coffee hadn't arrived on the ship. I didn't believe him. The shyster was trying to do me out of my cut, and after I took all the risk of acquiring the diamonds, hiding them, and shipping the coffee. He had no honor. I took him to task for failing to honor our agreement."

"Quite so. The fact remains, you have retrieved some of the diamonds he found in the fish tank. Others remain in the coffee, and it will be a job for two to sift them out. Since Boddy is out of the picture, what say you to a sixty-forty split, in my favor?"

"You're forgetting I did all the work of acquisition and delivery. Seventy-thirty split, in my favor."

"You're forgetting I know what happened to Boddy."

Colonel Mustard stared hard at the bag of coffee beans. "Fifty-fifty, and that's my final offer."

"Agreed." Green offered his hand. Mustard took it with a firm shake.

"Well, to work then, sifting through this lot." Mustard pointed at the sack.

"Yes, and please, let's not ruin the beans in the process," Green said. "Some of us need real coffee."

They set to work, sifting and sorting. The tiny collection of uncut diamonds grew into a modest handful.

Green grinned to himself as he worked. They'd split the diamonds equally. After they'd hidden them in their rooms, they'd accidentally discover Boddy in the conservatory and alert the authorities.

When everyone was in turmoil, their minds focused on the tragic event, he'd take a little stroll through the kitchen garden and spend some time rooting through the compost heap. Fifty-fifty only applied to the diamonds in the coffee sack.

THE WATER SUITE

"I say, is he dead?" Professor Plum swallowed. He had never seen a dead person, well, except those wrapped in mummy cloths who had been dead three thousand years. Never a fresh body lying in a tumble on a kitchen floor beside a sink.

"Possibly." Poke, poke. "Yes, quite. Stand clear." Colonel Mustard swept his riding crop through the air above the body, as if he was clearing away invisible spectators, or casting a spell.

Professor Plum stepped back. "I'll, um, well, I suppose we should, um, I don't know."

"The first thing we do is look for clues. I suspect that wrench lying there has something to do with the gash on his head."“

"I suppose you're right. What's a wrench doing here?" Plum glanced around the kitchen. The pipes under the sink had been taken apart, and a heap of sludge spewed out of the u-trap onto a pile of newspapers. A revolting aroma emanated from the grey slime. "Do you suppose Boddy had been doing a spot of do-it-yourself plumbing?"

"Doesn't seem likely. They have tradesmen for that sort of thing. Perhaps an itinerant plumber came to fix the pipes, got into a row with Boddy about the workmanship, and clubbed him."

"That sounds plausible, Mustard. Move to the top of the class for intuitive thinking. But I wonder about that." Plum pointed to something glittery under Boddy's hand.

Mustard reached out with his riding crop and flicked the suspect item free. It skittered across the tiles and stopped near Plum's foot.

He picked it up. "It's an earring. Purplish-blue enamel dolphin leaping out of diamond waves. Why would a tradesman, who is unlikely to be paid for this particular job, leave a valuable earring at the scene?"

"Perhaps you ought to take a closer look at it. Authenticate it."

"Yes, I will. When I have my magnifying glass." Plum slipped the earring in his pocket. "Do you suppose the tradesman was a woman, and she dropped her earring and hasn't realized it yet? She can hardly come back, can she, and ask for it?"

"Highly unlikely, my boy. A woman in the trades. Ought not to be allowed. Unseemly for the fair sex to be messing about with pipes." Mustard smoothed his row of medals. "Is there anything else lying about that might lead us to unmasking this nefarious tradesman?"

"Only the pipe and the sludge. Looks like Boddy was cleaning out a blockage." Plum watched a slow drip fall from the open drain in the sink into a small but growing pool on the floor. "I suppose we won't get dinner now, with the sink being out of commission."

"Here, here, this won't do. Can't have the kitchen less than shipshape. I imagine you're a dab hand with tools. Fix it."

Plum looked down at his tweeds. "Not in these clothes. I'll have to change into my field outfit."

"Go and do that now, chappie, while I call the authorities. We'll need to get this unfortunate incident cleared away by teatime." Mustard tapped his riding crop on the tiles for emphasis.

Plum slunk away. Imagine having to clean drains. Still, someone had to do it. Mustard clearly thought he was in charge and above doing actual work. Green would slither his way out of it, and they'd be left without meals. So it was all on his shoulders. He climbed the stairs, changed into his older pants and shirt, and picked up his magnifying glass. No point in hurrying. The drain wasn't going anywhere. He sat by the window and studied the earring carefully. The enamel was of fairly good quality, but the rows of diamond waves were clearly paste. The earring was a bit of costume jewelry, nothing more.

He left the earring on his night table, tucked the magnifying glass in his pocket, and returned to the kitchen. A dirty job awaited him, but he'd spent many happy hours sifting through dirt in Egypt. He'd treat this the same way. Perhaps there was a discovery to be made. He rolled up his sleeves as he walked down the passageway and nearly bumped into Mrs. Peacock who was leaving the dining room.

"Oh, you frightened me," she said, one hand clutched at her throat. Between her fingers a diamond necklace winked at him. "Such a dreadful business in the kitchen. I've told Mrs. White to slip in now and make some tea, before the police chase her out. She'll have to bring water down from upstairs, I suppose, but it can't be helped. We'll need some sustenance before this day is through."

He nodded. A cup of tea with a selection of shortbread and tarts would be a fine reward upon completion of his imminent task.

In the kitchen he found Colonel Mustard on guard over the body, and Mrs. White fussing around the Aga cooker.

"There'll be no more tea here today until I get that sink back. How am I to wash the cups after, I ask you?" She slapped the kettle onto the stovetop and began filling a tray with saucers. "My late Winslow, rest his soul, would have had that sink fixed in a trice. I asked Mr. Boddy after lunch, when it backed up, to call someone. He got on the telephone, but he didn't call a plumber. He called some school. I don't want an apprentice messing about. I want someone who knows his job."

Mustard harrumphed. "Plum's the man. Might not be a plumber but he knows how to do an honest day's work. Stand clear, now. Let the man through."

Plum sat down on the floor next to the u-trap. "So this was blocked? Boddy was trying to clear it?"

"Aye, that's the sad tale of it. And me with dinner to make and spuds to wash."

That was news to lift his heart from his unsavory task. Potatoes for dinner. She was making mashed potatoes. He'd be able to eat. He took a knife from the counter and poked at the sludge in the drain. If he didn't clear it out, the sink would back up again. The sludge smelled vile. It smelled like the remains of a dozen Mrs. White dinners. He'd need a walk in the fresh air after he was finished this task. At least he didn't have to catalogue it.

He poked and prodded until a large irregular chunk fell out. A sharp pin stuck out from it, and was the likely culprit, preventing the object from sweeping away with the dishwater. With care for his hands, he laid the offending object on a piece of newspaper and wrapped it up.

"That's cleared it, Mrs. White," he said, scraping the rest of the sludge from the inside of the pipe. "Looks like a bit of broken crockery. I'll have the pipe back on in a few minutes."

"Broken crockery. That Miss Scarlet was in here earlier looking for coffee. I expect she broke a cup and tried to hide it. You'll be taking that mess out to the compost heap when you're done. I'll be all afternoon trying to clear the stench."

Plum wrapped the remaining sludge in a newspaper and passed it to Mustard. “Here, the sooner this is outside, the sooner we’ll all be able to breathe again.”

Mustard grumbled but he took the package outside.

Using Boddy’s wrench, Plum reattached the pipe. “There, good as new. You might want to keep a bucket under here, in case it leaks. Will the tea be long?”

“Just a few minutes. I’ll bring it to the lounge.”

“Good. I’ll go and clean up.” Plum walked calmly away from the kitchen, but hastened his steps in the passageway and up the stairs to his room. Inside, he closed the door and opened a window. Then he unwrapped the parcel from the drain. It was no piece of crockery. He’d never seen a tea cup with a pin attached. Gently he wiped the goo off with the corner of the newspaper. As he thought. It was a brooch. A big one.

A little rinse under the taps while he washed his hands and it would be good as new. And it was. A purplish-blue enamel fish swimming through a diamond sea dotted with emerald seaweed. Or was it?

A few minutes with his magnifying glass revealed the diamonds and emeralds were paste.

He hid it under his pillow.

The gong rang announcing tea in the lounge.

Plum changed back to his regular clothes and hurried downstairs.

“I’ll help you with the dishes, Mrs. White,” Miss Scarlet was saying. “I’m sure you must be under a great deal of stress today. And the kitchen smells much better now.” She stretched out on the chesterfield so there was barely room for her mother who sat at the other end.

Colonel Mustard hurried in. “Hope I’m not too late. Bit of a holdup in the kitchen, explaining about the vagabond tradesman. Did you get that crockery washed up, Plum? I noticed the package I took to the compost was soupy, not lumpy." He settled himself into one of the green leather chairs.

"Have you been making soup, Plum?" Green asked, turning from the window where he was admiring the lawn.

"No, just helping Mrs. White by replacing the drain Boddy removed." Plum sat in the second green leather chair quickly, before he lost it to Green.

"Not Boddy," Mustard said. "A tradesman."

"Poor Boddy." Mrs. Peacock ran her finger around her necklace, a bluish-purple enamel seashell floating on multiple strands of diamonds. "Such a dreadful affair."

They all stared into their cups for a few minutes. Plum sorely needed a refill but was afraid to break the silence. Miss Scarlet took off an earring and rubbed her earlobe. She placed the earring on the table beside her. Plum stared at it. A cluster of red stones around a gold center. He looked to the table at the other end of the chesterfield. An earring sat there beside the lamp. Purplish-blue enamel dolphin leaping out of diamond waves.

"Who'd be after having a bit of shortbread with the tea?" Mrs. White asked from her post, standing next to the mantel, arms folded over her apron. "Now that I've got kitchen help, I can afford to pass out plates."

Miss Scarlet looked alarmed. "Oh dear, I've offered to help and I've forgotten all about my manicure. So sorry." She shrugged and held up her fingernails, displaying the red enamel finish.

"That didn't bother you earlier when you were mucking in the sink. I don't know what you broke and tried to flush away, but I'll know when I count the cups."

"I didn't break anything. Really. The sink problem had nothing to do with me."

Plum stared at the two earrings on the two tables. Why would she leave them lying around? "That's a nice earring, that red one," he said. "Aren't you afraid you'll lose it?"

Miss Scarlet glanced at it. "Oh, I'm always losing earrings. I take them off if they pinch. That one's dreadful. My ear's throbbing."

Green strolled from his position at the window to the shortbread tray on the table near Mrs. Peacock. On route, Plum saw him scoop the purplish-blue earring into his pocket. No wonder Miss Scarlet was always losing them. Green probably had a healthy collection by now.

"It must cost a fortune if you have to replace your earrings frequently," Plum said.

"Not if you buy the cheap ones," Mrs. Peacock said. "Or help yourself."

"I see you've helped yourself to my jewel box, Mother," Miss Scarlet said. "You've probably lost the earrings that match that necklace."

"No, they weren't there, and you know how I hate to be mismatched. Besides, this necklace is not your color."

"Perhaps if you gave me a more substantial allowance I wouldn't have to wear cheap jewelry that didn't accessorize my clothes."

"Perhaps if you'd stayed in school until graduation you might be better off."

Plum hunkered down in his seat. He hated family bickering.

"Did you not finish school, Miss Scarlet?" Mr. Green asked. "It's a sin to waste a fine mind."

"Miss Puce didn't see any point in me continuing when I had an acting job waiting with Midnight Smoke."

Mrs. Peacock made a strangled coughing noise.

Mrs. White shook her head. "That's not the way I heard it. Master Boddy and I were discussing the matter just yesterday. I heard Miss Puce tossed you out."

"Midnight Smoke is hardly a respectable theater company."

"You just never wanted me to be a successful actress, Mother. You don't want me to be famous." Miss Scarlet pouted.

"Depends what you mean by famous." Mrs. Peacock ran her finger along the diamond waves of her necklace. "You've been in the tabloids for weeks. That's fame for you."

Plum slipped out of the room. He couldn't abide listening to any more sniping. He went to the study, where Boddy had made his telephone call. Boddy's notepad had a telephone number written on it, identified as *Miss Puce's School for Girls*. Beside it he'd written *Water Suite. Line is busy.*

Plum imagined him coming to the study to find a plumber for the blockage. Did Miss Puce's curriculum include a Trades elective?

He pondered that as he returned to his room. He pulled out the brooch and the earring. They were related in theme and stones, but he didn't know if they belonged together. He wasn't much up on women's accessories. He studied them again with his magnifying glass. Definitely paste.

He stepped over to the wastebasket where he had tossed the newspaper he'd used to wrap the brooch to smuggle it upstairs. It was an old one, a single page yellowed and brittle. It looked like it had been taken from a scrapbook. There were bits of glue on the back. He smoothed it out as carefully as a mummy's shroud. It featured a photo of a group of people in suits.

The caption read: *TOP SCHOOLS HONOR SCHOLARS. England's top scholars were feted today in a ceremony at Obsidian College. Pictured, left to right, are the headmasters and their scholars. Headmaster Inkk of Obsidian College with John Boddy, Headmistress Puce of Miss Puce's School for Girls with Rose Currant, and Headmaster Dunn of Roan Hills with Ginger Bricke.*

All the participants were dressed to the nines, with pocket watches gleaming and diamonds glinting. There was not a smudged shoe in the group. Plum took a good look at Miss Puce, in her best clothes and her finest jewelry, with his magnifying glass. Yes, it was all becoming clear.

He returned to the lounge, where the bickering continued, and pointed his magnifying glass. "I accuse you of killing Mr. Boddy in the kitchen with the wrench."

The Water Suite

Solution:

"I accuse you of stealing my jewelry," Miss Scarlet shot back at him. "I found my earring in your room. You were going to sell it and keep the money."

"I was not. I was only examining it."

"Is it worth anything?" Green asked.

"Well, I never!" Mrs. White said, thrusting hands on hips. "Young ladies going into the gentlemen's bedrooms, and gentlemen stealing from the other guests. And someone killing the host. Well, I never!"

"I can explain, really I can," Plum said. If only they would listen for a few minutes, instead of going off on tangents. "I think you'll find an item of interest in Green's pocket. Green thought it might be worth something, but of course, it's not. That's why you're still wearing them. The suite of jewelry you stole from Miss Puce. It was her favorite. She called it the Water Suite. That's why you were expelled."

"Mr. Green? Is this true? Are you stealing my earrings too?" Miss Scarlet asked, fingering her ear with one hand and scooping her errant red earring off the end table with the other.

Professor Plum clapped his hands twice. "Please try to pay attention. If I could recount the facts. This morning Miss Scarlet was in the kitchen, seeking coffee. Mr. Boddy noticed she was wearing a brooch that strongly resembled the one stolen from Miss Puce. He remembered it from a newspaper clipping which he produced from his scrapbook and showed her. He asked her to give the brooch back. Miss Scarlet refused. Mr. Boddy threatened to call Miss Puce. When he returned to the kitchen, he found Miss Scarlet had dropped the piece down the drain. Mrs. White had tried to use the sink, and the wastewater backed up. Boddy got out a wrench to retrieve it. At the first opportunity after he removed the drainpipe, Miss Scarlet whacked him on the head with the wrench. She would have retrieved her brooch but the stench was too strong."

"All that for a suite of poorly matched costume jewelry," Mrs. Peacock said. "If it wasn't for the nautical theme and similar stones, it wouldn't match at all. Didn't I tell you to get rid of it as soon as I found it in your case? I knew you had stolen it. I'd had to visit Miss Puce on more than one occasion to discuss your behavior, and she was always wearing one or the other bits of it."

"Miss Puce said they were real diamonds," Miss Scarlet protested.

"Of course she did." Mrs. Peacock sniffed. "She fancied herself as rich and elegant."

"School marms don't wear diamonds," Mrs. White muttered.

Plum sat back in his chair. Let them argue all they want. He had brought the truth to the fore.

On the other side of the room, Green slipped something small out of his pocket and into a bowl of candies.

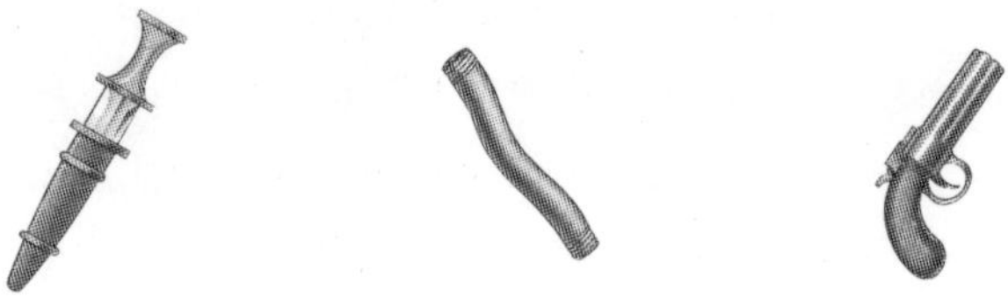

One Tin Soldier

Miss Scarlet stood at the lounge window gazing over the driveway and the lawns. She was so bored. Bored, bored, bored. Bored hanging about with these old codgers and her mother. Six weeks in a Hampshire mansion, a summer lolling around in the stodgy old rooms, swimming in the decrepit swimming pool, drinking tea with fools. And it was only the first week in June, with five more weeks to go. What to do?

Ah, here was something. The postman ambled up the driveway with a bundle of packages and letters. He looked a bit of all right, with black curly hair under his postman's cap, and a swing in his step. Mother would say he was beneath her station, but there was nothing wrong with a mild flirtation to fill in a dead spot in the afternoon.

She turned away from the window and checked her appearance in the small mirror on the wall. Hair, perfect, as usual. Maybe just a little plumping near her cheeks, to make the curls fall properly. Makeup, perfect, just the right shade of vermilion lipstick to match her dress and shoes. No lipstick on her teeth. No cracked fingernail polish, she'd spent an hour on her nails today. All she needed was something to say. *Hello, I'm Josephine, and you are…?* No, a little too forward. *Hello, do you come here often?* Well, silly, he was the postman. He came every day. *Lovely weather for a walk, isn't it?* Good enough.

She sashayed out of the lounge into the entrance hall, with just the right swing in her hips to make her dress swish around her knees.

Drat. Too late. The post had been pushed through the slot and lay in a heap on the floor. She opened the door and peered down the drive. Yes, there he was, striding off to finish his rounds. Maybe tomorrow.

But he'd left two packages on the step. She picked them up. Modest boxes, one fairly heavy, both addressed to John Boddy.

John would be in his study, he spent every afternoon in the study working on the plans for his birthday party. He didn't have much time to spend with his guests. Too bad, as he was young and handsome and interesting. Not to mention rich.

She carried the post to the study and knocked on the door.

"Come in."

"Hello, John," she said, swirling her skirts to his desk. "Here's the post. You got two parcels. How exciting! I wonder what's in them."

He grunted, put down his pen, and took the parcels from her hands. Cutting through the string with a small ivory-handled knife, he opened the smaller, lighter one first. It contained a bundle of old letters tied up in red ribbon, and a folded sheet of paper. He opened the sheet, and she read over his shoulder.

My dear Mr. Boddy,

Following the recent death of my mother, Maude Clippenden, I was sorting through her possessions and came across this bundle of letters sent to her by my father, Captain Jeffery Clippenden, of the Royal Hampshire Regiment, the Tigers, while he was stationed in the Sudan during Lord Kitchener's wars.

In them, Father speaks highly of Sir Hugh Black, an officer with the

Tigers. As you are his heir, I write to you for assistance. I know you would want to do everything in your power to honor a soldier who served with your illustrious uncle.

I have enclosed the letters for your review. As you can see, they are an outstanding account of one man's war. I trust you will find them as engrossing as I, and will agree they ought to be published. As I am without the means to accomplish this, I implore you to take up my cause and seek an appropriate publisher so my father's story will not be lost in the mists of time.

Your obedient servant,

Matilda Clippenden

"That looks interesting, John. Are you going to accept? Colonel Mustard and Professor Plum could help you. They've both dealt with publishers." She ran her finger along the pile of old envelopes. They were yellowed and torn open. The last one was stained with something brownish.

"First, I'd have to see what dreary story the man has to tell. I've received these before. They're usually most monotonous." Boddy pushed the letters to one side and opened the second box with his small knife. It contained two smaller boxes.

"Are they shoes? They could be shoes." Miss Scarlet held her breath. Shoes. She could spend hours trying on shoes.

He removed the lid from the first smaller box. Inside lay an entire regiment of tin soldiers, outfitted in bright red uniforms.

"Toy soldiers! How wonderful! Do you collect them? Can you play with them? I've never played with tin soldiers before; is it fun? Oh, do come and play with me, John."

"Go play with them yourself; I'm busy." He pushed the box of toys into her hands and turned back to the package of letters. He untied the red ribbon, pulled the first letter out of its envelope, and began reading.

Miss Scarlet thought about stamping her feet and pouting to get him to change his mind, but thought better of it. War was so boring. Playing at war with tin soldiers would be appallingly tedious.

She carried the box into the billiard room and perched it on the edge of the billiard table. She could use the soldiers to set up a diorama of a Coco Chanel fashion show. She could cut dresses from colored paper and glue them to the little men. Or she could set them up in a Noel Coward play and read the script as she moved them through the scenes. This could be fun. Certainly more fun than sitting in the lounge listening to Mother prattle about insufficient funds.

It didn't take long to unpack all the soldiers. There were two groups of them, one red and one blue. Most of them carried little rifles. A bunch knelt down on one knee, shooting, while another bunch marched with rifles on shoulders. There were several little drummer boys, bugle boys, and flag bearers. Two carried big swords. Three were sitting at tables signing papers. Four were wearing little cooks' aprons and holding tiny wooden spoons. There was a collection of cannons. There were no horses. That was a shame, as she rather liked horses, but there wouldn't be any in her fashion show diorama, so perhaps it was just as well.

She began lining them up, creating a catwalk out of cue chalk boxes and placing spectators on either side. She placed the half-kneeling soldiers here and there around the catwalk to act as photographers. She placed the more decorative soldiers on the catwalk, and stood back to consider how she might dress them.

"Let me guess, the Battle of Mafeking?" Colonel Mustard asked.

He had slipped in rather quietly, as she hadn't noticed. "No, it's Coco Chanel's opening in Paris last year."

'Twaddle." Colonel Mustard reached out his riding crop and swept her figures off the catwalk. "These are soldiers. You disgrace the uniform by playing at fashion shows. These figures should be set in a battlefield diorama."

"But I don't know any battles."

"As it happens, I do. I rather think the Battle of El Obeid in the Sudan in 1898 was an interesting one. I was awarded the Obeid Star for that. The Queen herself presented it. Only survivor of my detachment. I'd have been a goner if the General hadn't shown up on the flanks." He pulled the soldiers over to one corner of the billiard table. "Let me show you how it unfolded. Imagine this is a long dry valley, and these are the hills of Kordofan." He placed billiard balls along the sides of his designated valley. "Over here we have our encampment, with tents and a stone mission we had taken over as hospital and stores." He placed two chalk boxes to represent the buildings, and perched his folded hanky as a tent.

Miss Scarlet sorted through the men to find an officer sitting at a table. She placed him under the tent. This might actually be fun. The Colonel's stories were usually egregiously boring, but the live action scene could be interesting. "That's you, in charge."

"Alas, I was only a captain then. That would be our Major, who was killed later, as you shall see."

"I say, what's going on here?" Professor Plum leaned over the billiard table. "Is this a new game of billiards? With obstacles?"

"No, the colonel is arranging a diorama of a famous battle."

"Jolly good fun, I should say. May we watch? I'll get the others." He scurried away and returned some minutes later with Boddy, Mrs. Peacock, and Mr. Green. “Mrs. White says she’s too busy to be playing about with toys, but she’s promised to deliver four o’clock tea here if we like. Carry on, Colonel.”

“As I was saying, our detachment of the Royal Hampshires, the Tigers, was garrisoned at the El Obeid mission, tracking the movements of the Sudanese.” He placed a handful of soldiers around the tent and a few on the roofs of the chalk boxes. “At dawn, our sentry reported enemy movement in the hills.” He paused here and placed dozens of the little blue soldiers behind the billiard balls. “They weren’t in blue, of course, they were in white gowns and turbans, while we were in our khakis, but red and blue is all we have for toy soldiers, I’m afraid.”

“They look pretty against the green billiard table,” Miss Scarlet said.

“As I was saying, we had a quick conference in the command tent, and I decided we ought to make our stand on the roof of the mission buildings.” He trotted a couple of the soldiers to the tent, then trotted them to the chalk boxes.

“I can’t keep track of which one is you, Colonel,” Plum said. “They all look the same.”

“Let me help.” Mrs. Peacock took off her multicolored feathered hat, selected a mustard-yellow feather, plucked it free, and looped it through the tiny arms of the sword-carrying officer like a stole. “There, that’s Colonel Mustard.”

“Right-y ho,” Mustard said, taking the little figure of himself and moving it to the front ranks. “This is how it looked. Imagine this. Dawn. Sun rising over rust-colored hills. They had us surrounded. They came swooping down from the hills and charging our walls. We were up on the roof, shooting in all directions. They were shooting and throwing spears.

Men were dropping all around me. I knew I should be lucky to see it out. I was the highest ranking officer on the roof. The men looked to me for command. I encouraged them to fight on, as the enemy swarmed toward us. For every one we shot, two more appeared from behind a rock. We were using the Lee-Metford magazine rifle, which had replaced the single-loading Martini-Henry. . . ."

Miss Scarlet felt her eyes glaze over. What was that he said? Magazine? Was there a magazine for guns, like there was a magazine for hats and several for fashion? Did the soldiers gather around the campfire looking at the latest in side arms and reading gun etiquette? She should have insisted on carrying on with her fashion show diorama. This was all too tedious. She glanced at Mother, whose face wore that set expression that makes you think she's here but she's really miles away.

"And that's what happened. I was most relieved to see the General riding in from the northeast with another detachment, I can tell you. The Sudanese high-tailed it into the hills. The Tigers carried me out on their shoulders. I was sent back to England then, on leave, and had my meeting with the Queen."

"And I am most relieved to see it's four o'clock and Mrs. White is about to serve tea," Mrs. Peacock said. "Shall we retire to the lounge?"

Miss Scarlet glanced down at the tableau, to see all the soldiers lying dead on the chalk box roof, while the Colonel Mustard tin soldier stood alone up there, facing a bunch of drum and bugle soldiers marching toward him. She followed the others to the lounge. She was never so glad to sit down. The toy soldiers had started out as fun, but the colonel's monotone voice had nearly lulled her to sleep standing up. She was no closer to understanding the battle, but she was sure Coco Chanel's fashion show would have been much more interesting. Perhaps tomorrow she would slip into the billiard room and try again.

After dinner, she played a few hands of whist with Mother, Boddy and Plum, then begged off to bed.

The next day, she woke at noon to a clamor of voices. She threw on her crimson Chinese silk robe and matching slippers and followed the sounds to the billiard room.

They were all there, gathered around the billiard table.

"What's going on?" she asked, glancing at the toy soldiers. Good, they were still there, although they had been moved.

"Mr. Boddy's been stabbed." Plum pointed to the floor on the far side of the table. "He's dead."

Boddy lay against the leg of the table, a toy soldier in one hand and a small ivory-handled knife in his chest.

Miss Scarlet stepped back. She looked again at the diorama. All the soldiers from both sides had been moved to the billiard ball hills, and appeared to be engaged in hand-to hand combat. The figure wearing the yellow feather no longer commanded from the roof of the mission. He crouched under the table in the tent.

"Stand clear, now. Don't touch anything. I'll take charge." Colonel Mustard shoed them all out with his riding crop. "I've sent for the authorities. Keep the area clear."

Miss Scarlet joined the others in the march to the dining room, where Mrs. White had thoughtfully provided tea and currant scones to soothe the emotions.

"What happened? Did anyone hear anything?"

"If you'd get out of bed at a reasonable hour you wouldn't have to ask," Mrs. Peacock said. "After breakfast I spoke to Boddy about our cuisine. Then I went to the kitchen and had a talk with Mrs. White about the possibility of making beef bourguignon for dinner. I spent some time explaining it. I do hope she understood. She seemed quite keen on it."

"We'll be lucky," Mr. Green said.

"I suppose your time was better spent this morning?" Mrs. Peacock asked, her feather hair ornament quivering.

"As a matter of fact, I spent some time talking to Boddy about the need for a chapel built onto the mansion. I suggested he commission me to do the planning and supervise the construction. He said he was too busy to think about it at the moment, but I could broach the subject again after his birthday. So I went to the library and looked for some examples of adequate architecture."

"I talked to him this morning, too," Plum said. "I asked if he knew of any openings in the anthropology field. He's quite connected, you know. He said he might have a little job for me, writing the memoirs of a soldier. He gave me a packet of letters to work on. I can hardly wait to get started. I spent the rest of the morning in my room, gathering pens and paper. I'm that chuffed." He grinned at them.

Miss Scarlet munched on a scone. What she wouldn't give for a strong cup of coffee. She was in for another boring day, with Mother on a tear about beef, Green playing about with chapels, and Plum working on those tedious letters. She'd have to take a long luxurious bath. That would fill in the afternoon.

When she reappeared, refreshed and dressed in a clingy dress of strawberry chiffon, in case that postman happened by, the lounge was empty. She heard Mother's voice drifting from the kitchen, a cadence of words lilting with beef, beef, beef. Best not to go there, even if she was desperate for coffee.

Men's voices reverberated from the library. She wandered in to see what they were up to.

Colonel Mustard sat in the window seat in the bay window overlooking the ornamental shrubs, tapping the hardwood with his riding crop. Tap, tap, tap, like he was keeping time with some regimental marching song playing in his head. Plum occupied a seat at the long table, surrounded with papers and pens. A bundle of letters tied up in red ribbon sat directly in front of him. Green thumbed his way along the bookshelves, reading titles and pulling out the odd book to flip through.

"I say, Miss Scarlet, what do you think?" Plum asked.

"Think? About what?"

"About the title of this memoir I'm writing. A good title is most important. How about *A Soldier's Story*. Or *My Regiment's History*? Or something more personal: *Clippenden: One Man's War*."

"I'd say you'd be better off opening the letters first and seeing what he has to say," Green muttered. "Maybe he'll tell you *How I Won the War*."

Colonel Mustard tapped more briskly. "No need. No need at all. Toss the letters. Clippenden was a Tiger. I can recount the Tiger's story, chapter and verse. You can call it *Heroes Among Tigers*. I remember the time the regiment was stationed in Rangoon…"

"What do you say, Miss Scarlet?" Plum asked, as Colonel Mustard droned on behind him.

She sat down near Plum and reached for the packet of letters. It would be like reading old newspapers, but it would fill in the time. "I say it wouldn't hurt to read a couple first, see what they're all about." She pulled at the ribbon, and the packet fell apart.

"Oh, dear, must keep them in order, most important to be methodical." He scooped them into an orderly pile and proceeded to number the envelopes consecutively. "There. One hundred and two letters. I shall be busy for weeks. I hope the estate will pay me for my time. Or the publisher will advance me something in anticipation. You received an advance for your memoirs, didn't you, Colonel?"

"I did. See here, Plum, this Clippenden was just a foot soldier. No need to trouble yourself with his account. I'll dispose of those if you like. I know the real story."

Plum threw his body over the letters just as Mustard's riding crop came sweeping across the table. Mustard stalked out.

"What's the matter with him?" Miss Scarlet asked.

"He needs to provide his publisher with a manuscript, and there's one almost written in those letters," Green said. "He's looking for the easy way out. The Lord helps those who help themselves to the work of others."

Plum scowled. "I'll keep close tabs on this lot, then. He can write his own story. I'll write this one. We'll see who gets to the publisher first."

He picked up envelope number one and opened it, carefully transcribing the number 'one' on the pages of the letter, and recording on his papers the date and time he had opened it. He settled back to read.

Miss Scarlet sighed. What could be more boring, watching Green flip though ancient books, or watching Plum read yellowed letters with too much protocol? At least Mustard wasn't thumping out a beat any longer.

She stared at the pile of letters. She could make a game out of this. See if she could purloin a letter from the stack without Plum noticing. She'd learned a few things about pilfering at Miss Puce's School for Girls. She leaned forward in her seat, resting her arms on the tabletop, and began moving her fingers toward the pile with stealth while watching Plum's eyes. He was completely absorbed in his reading. Inch by inch, her fingers closed in on the quarry.

"Oh, listen to this," Plum said. "It says 'We were stationed in a dreary old shack with dreary old rations and not so much as a pack of cards between us.' Isn't that fascinating? Clippenden certainly had a way with words."

Miss Scarlet took full advantage of his reading aloud. While he focused on reading the words, she snagged the bottom letter from the pile. This was too easy. He was such a ninny. She could have this letter concealed in chiffon and out the library door in a trice. Too, too easy. More challenging would be to open the letter and read it right here in front of him. See if he noticed.

Silently she slipped the missive from the envelope. Quietly she unfolded the pages and smoothed them flat. Plum didn't look up. She had Green's full attention, though. He was poised at the end of a row of books, one hand on a dusty volume, his eyes on her, a smirk on his face. She flashed him a grin. He winked. She carried on.

The letter began in a firm hand.

Dearest Maude,

I fear we are in a dangerous spot. Captain Mustard and I have conferred about the situation and disagree on the right course of action. The Sudanese are filtering down through the hills; we can see their lights winking in the dark. By dawn we'll be surrounded. I say we attack now, take them by surprise. Mustard says we ought to make a run for it, down the valley toward Khartoum. The General is approaching with reinforcements from that direction. I think we can't afford to abandon our post to the enemy.

The letter continued in pencil, in a shaky hand.

It is almost dawn. For lack of a consensus, I took charge of the men and ordered an attack. We are poised to creep out of our position and attack the largest group of the enemy in the hills directly to the northwest. Mustard assures me the General and his troops are but an hour away. We shall fight like Tigers. I march behind the Major at the point of our wedge, taking my men where I do not fear to go. I don't see Mustard, who should be in the second column. Last I saw him he was in the tent messing around with his pen. The major is one of the first to fall.

Miss Scarlet slid the letter back in the yellowed envelope. This didn't sound like the battle the Colonel had described. Maybe she wasn't paying enough attention yesterday to the interminable story. There was something else wrong, too, but she couldn't quite put her finger on it. Maybe if she took a walk, she'd remember.

She stood up and walked to the door. When she looked back, Plum hadn't even noticed she'd gone.

Out in the passageway she wondered where she should go to jog her memory. The billiard room was quiet. The police had come and gone. She went in and stood looking down at the little diorama. Just as the letter said, the soldiers were clumped at the hills, a flying wedge of little red soldiers shooting at the little blue soldiers behind the rocks. Someone had laid most of the soldiers on their backs, to indicate they had been shot. One of the red soldiers was lying on a tiny scrap of paper torn from a notepad. A column of blue soldiers marched toward the chalk box buildings, but veered off because a contingent of flags, bugles, and drums was marching toward them from the northeast. A sword-bearing officer led them. He must be the General.

But where was the little tin soldier with the feather stole? Not in the hills. Not on the chalk box roof where he was positioned earlier. No, he was in the tent, under the table.

How very strange. She hadn't paid attention to much of Mustard's story, but she was sure the figure with the feather fought from the roof.

She wandered away. All this thinking made her head hurt. She really needed some coffee. The door to the study was open. She'd sit in there for a moment before she challenged the kitchen.

Boddy's desk was much as she had seen it yesterday. She sat in his desk chair. The brown paper wrap from the two packages was on the floor under the desk. A pile of papers on the desk blotter concerned the ordering of flowers and musicians for the birthday party. A piece of notepaper missing a corner lay on top. It said *Home Office* and listed a telephone number, in Boddy's precise handwriting.

Something yellowed poked out from under the blotter. She pulled it out. It was an old envelope, stained with something brownish. That's what she couldn't remember. The pile of letters Boddy had received had one dirty one at the bottom of the pile. This letter.

She opened it.

Dearest Maude,

The enemy has mistaken me for dead. They are marching past us, toward our field station. I am weak with pain and loss of blood. No one else is moving. I can hear the General's bugles in the distance. They are coming to save us. I hope I stay alive long enough to tell them Mustard didn't join. . . .

The last word trailed off.

Miss Scarlet returned the letter to its envelope and strode to the library. Mrs. White was serving a tray of something to the men and Mother.

She stopped at the foot of the long table, pointing with the stained letter.

"I accuse you of killing John Boddy in the billiard room with the knife."

One Tin Soldier

Solution:

Professor Plum looked up and blinked. "Me? Why would I do that? Boddy offered me a job writing these memoirs. He was going to pay me."

"Not you, silly. You. Colonel Mustard." She pointed her letter over Plum's head, at the colonel, tap-tap-tapping his beat on the hardwood again at the window seat.

"Preposterous." Tap. "Nonsense." Tap. "Poppycock." Tap.

"You told us all about the Battle of El Obeid. You demonstrated it to us on the billiard table. Captain Clippenden recounts it in his letters. Only his version and your version are different. Boddy watched you set the scene in toy soldiers. Then he read the letters. He gave the letters to Plum to write into a memoir. But he held back the last letter, as proof. He went back to the billiard room and showed you how the scene really went. He was going to call the Home Office and have your Obeid Star rescinded. Last man alive, extreme valor. The only reason you survived was you were hiding under the table in the command post tent."

"If I might explain. I fully intended to accompany Clippenden to the battle. I was just wrapping up my paperwork, and I dropped the cap of my fountain pen. I bent to pick it up, and at that moment the enemy fired a round of cannon. In the reverberation I banged my head on the underside of the table. When I regained consciousness, the battle was over and the General arriving. I ran out on the roof to wave at him."

Miss Scarlet sighed. Everybody had a version of this particular battle. She ought to have stuck with Coco Chanel.